Understanding My Church

Understanding My Church

Samuel J. Stoesz

Christian Publications, Inc.

Camp Hill, Pennsylvania

Christian Publications, Inc.
Publishing House of The Christian and Missionary Alliance
3825 Hartzdale Drive
Camp Hill, PA 17011-8870

The mark of  *vibrant faith*

Library of Congress Catalog Card Number: 82-73214
ISBN: 0-87509-325-6
First edition © 1968 by Christian Publications, Inc.
Revised edition © 1983 by Christian Publications, Inc.
Unless otherwise indicated, all quotations are taken from the
HOLY BIBLE: NEW INTERNATIONAL VERSION,
copyright © 1978 by the New York International Bible Society,
and are used by permission.
Printed in The United States of America

Contents

Understanding the Church's Historical Development

Understanding The Christian and Missionary Alliance in the Twentieth Century

Preface

The church of Jesus Christ is God's master strategy in this world in which we live. It is founded upon biblical principles that have been maintained in every century, for God so designed the church that it would advance the gospel and nurture converts into maturity as true disciples.

A clear understanding of the doctrine of the church is essential to the growth and effectiveness of the church. To reach that understanding in our day, we must have some sense of the history of the church and the preservation of the truth through the ages.

The principle of learning from the past is biblical, for the Word of God draws analogies, patterns, and lessons from the past to demonstrate the faithful providential working of God.

Someone has warned that "where the historical sense is least real, the theological construction is most empty." In these pages there is at least a bird's-eye view of the history of the church, and the pattern it provides to aid us in our understanding.

Understanding My Church has been prepared to provide a tool for teaching youth and adults about the church generally, and about The Christian and Missionary Alliance in particular. The original edition was published in 1968 at the request of the National Education Committee of The Christian and Missionary Alliance. Since that time the Alliance has undergone a series of reorganizational changes, necessitating this revised edition, but with the original purpose remaining unchanged.

UNDERSTANDING THE SCRIPTURAL CHURCH PATTERN

The definition of any community of God's people, local or otherwise, must be based on the nature and mission of Jesus Christ. While *Understanding My Church* explains the background and history of The Christian and Missionary Alliance, the reader should keep in mind that in Scripture the church, called the *body of Christ,* represents the life and mission of Jesus Christ in the world.

To understand more fully how God deals with man in and through the church today, we need to know how God dealt with man in the past. He made known His ways to man through the Old Testament prophets and prepared the way for Christ's coming and the New Testament church through His chosen people Israel. With a comprehensive background from the Old Testament we get a more accurate view of the church.

God never has left Himself without a witness regarding His relationship to men and nations (Acts 14:16-17). To this end God has given His divine revelation in the written and infallible Word of God (2 Tim. 3:15-17).

Interspersed in the Suffering-Servant passages of Isaiah 42—61 is a graphic description of who God's Christ (Messiah) would be when He came. This revelation of Jesus Christ was superimposed upon Israel as a suffering-servant people.

Listen to me, you islands; hear this you distant nations:

Before I was born the LORD called me; from my birth he has made mention of my name. ...

He said to me, "You are my servant, Israel, in whom I will display my splendor." . . .

"It is too small a thing for you to be my servant to restore the tribes of Jacob and bring back those of Israel I have kept.

I will also make you a light for the Gentiles,
that you may bring my salvation to the ends
of the earth" (Isa. 49:1, 3, 6).

God intended that the ministries of the suffering-servant community of Israel would benefit the
nations of the whole world. This was in keeping
with God's covenant with Abraham centuries
earlier: *and all peoples on earth will be blessed*
through you (Gen. 12:3).

Isaiah 50:4-6 is a further description of the Suffering Servant with the prophetic insight of Jesus'
own willingness to fulfill the Father's purpose:

The Sovereign LORD *has given me an in-*
structed tongue, to know the word that sus-
tains the weary. . . .

The Sovereign LORD *has opened my ears, and I*
have not been rebellious; I have not drawn
back.

> *I offered my back to those who beat me, my
> cheeks to those who pulled out my beard;
> I did not hide my face from mocking and spit-
> ting.*

A *servant* in this biblical usage was not a slave
who is inferior to another, but was one who has
given himself voluntarily to carry out fully the
purposes of another. He is so fully associated with
the master's understanding, sharing, agreement,
and commonness of will that he is identified with
him out of respect, honor, and love.

In this perspective, Israel, Jesus, and the church
are to be recognized as servants in God's purposes
in the world. Jesus is the perfect pattern of God's
intent for servanthood. When measured against
this model, Israel is seen as a failure. The church
should emulate Jesus for this is the scriptural
pattern.

1

The Church and Its Beginning

The beginning of the New Testament church is recognized as a major transition in history. The Suffering-Servant ministry of Jesus Christ in His life, death, and Resurrection made possible the nature of the church as a servant-people, even as God in His plan and wisdom had ordained. Truly, Pentecost was the outpouring of the Spirit of the victorious Christ!

The New Testament looks upon this all-significant transition as centered both in Jesus Christ, the God-man, and in what the cross represented. The Crucifixion lays the groundwork for both man's vertical relationship to God and horizontal relationship to others.

The "body" that was crucified on that cross and rose again was to be represented in a body of believers who would take the good news of reconciliation to the whole world.

Before the church in the New Testament can be viewed properly, however, its roots in the Old Testament must be remembered.

Remember that at that time you were separate from Christ, excluded from citizenship in Israel and foreigners to the covenants of the promise, without hope and without God in the world. But now in Christ Jesus you who once were far away have been brought near through the blood of Christ.

Consequently, you are no longer foreigners and aliens, but fellow citizens with God's people and members of God's household, built on the foundation of the apostles and prophets, with Christ Jesus himself as the chief cornerstone (Eph. 2:12-13, 19-20).

This cornerstone was Christ's own death and Resurrection and it relates to all of time and space comprehensively.

His intent was that now, through the church, the manifold wisdom of God should be made known to the rulers and authorities in the heavenly realms, according to his eternal purpose which he accomplished in Christ Jesus our Lord (Eph. 3:10-11).

The Old Testament Roots of the Church

Men have argued whether the church began at Pentecost or if it existed in the covenant of the Old Testament. The point the Apostle Paul makes in Ephesians is that a new transition in history occurred at the cross and the church is a central display cosmically and eternally. Certain features demonstrate the importance of Israel to this transition.

The New Testament believers as heirs with Israel

According to Ephesians 3:6, the Gentiles have been made *heirs together with Israel, members together of one body.* But this was only by grace through faith (Eph. 2:8-10).

In Deuteronomy 7:6-11, the Israelites were warned not to assume that they had been chosen because of any inherent goodness or wisdom on their part. They were reminded that their fathers—Abraham, Isaac, and Jacob—had entered into a covenant with God to raise up a servant-people through whom the nations of the earth were to be blessed and that God intended to fulfill that promised covenant.

Unfortunately, the history of Israel in the Old Testament from Exodus to the Chronicles is checkered with failings and restorations. God provided for Israel prophets, priests, a sacrificial system, moral and ceremonial laws, the tabernacle, and, later, the temple, all of which were designed to solicit their personal faith in God and the promises that were yet to be fulfilled. Though often Israel failed miserably to respond to God's promises and provisions, whenever they prayed and sought the face of God, He forgave them and intervened to help them out of the dire circumstances they had created for themselves (graphically depicted in Ps. 105-106).

In spite of all the ups and downs, God carried forward a revelation of His plan and purpose for the world. He also left a record of His faithfulness through His prophets for all who would believe His promises and enter into His plan and purpose as heirs together in one body.

The New Testament believers as members of the body

The Old Testament "body" was viewed in terms of a "nation" or a "kingdom," with the children of Israel as its people and the land of promise as its location. God ordained Israel as a servant-people through whom the seed, Jesus Christ, should come.

The death and Resurrection of Jesus Christ accomplished a redemptive work by which faith in Him would result in a body of believers, henceforth called "the church." This body would be united not on a basis of natural heirship or national boundaries as the nation of Israel, but on mutual faith.

Christ's victory over sin and death fulfilled all that was foreshadowed in the Old Testament. The *heirs together with Israel, members together of one body* (Eph. 3:6), now had a basis for fellowship unencumbered by political, racial, and social barriers.

The New Testament believers as sharers in the promise

The Apostle Paul felt it was essential that the church should see the whole panorama of God's purpose:

In reading this, then, you will be able to understand my insight into the mystery of Christ, . . . that through the gospel the Gentiles are heirs together with Israel, members together of one body, and sharers together in the promise in Christ Jesus (Eph. 3:4-6).

The early church understood itself as a part of prophecy and fulfillment. Christ himself emphasized the continuity and consistency of prophecy (Luke 24:44-45). The early

21

church, therefore, having recognized Him as the Suffering Servant, saw itself as a servant-people called to fulfill a plan that reached back to the beginning and looked forward to the coming again of Christ in His glory.

Peter, on the day of Pentecost, recognized fulfillment of promise and associated the whole panorama of Old Testament history with the prophecy of Joel (2:28-29). Using the *keys of the kingdom* promised by Christ (Matt. 16:19), he initiated a call for salvation and for baptism according to Christ's commission (Matt. 28:18-20). That day the new covenant or testament foretold by Jeremiah (31:31-34) was declared as in force.

The New Testament is the expression of faith accepted by the church as its standard of precept and practice. The Old Testament is viewed not as a mere canceled fulfillment, but as an authoritative document full of prophetic meaning. Peter, in his epistle addressed *to God's elect, strangers in the world, scattered, . . .* used words that Moses addressed to Israel (Exod. 19:6). He wrote:

> *You are a chosen people, a royal priesthood, a holy nation, a people belonging to God, that you may declare the praises of him who called you out of darkness into his wonderful light* (1 Pet. 2:9).

Thus, the New Testament church is a fellow partaker of the promise in Christ Jesus through the gospel.

The New Testament Image of the Church

The word *church* conjures up many widely differing images in today's world. Like Israel, the church through the centuries has had its failings and restorations, its ups and downs. But despite its many weaknesses and tragic sins, the church in every century since its inception has been the most powerful force for good in the world because it is God's designed instrument of His plan and purpose.

Jesus declared that He would build His church upon a rock and that the gates of hell would not overcome it (Matt. 16:18). The apostles were given the task to develop in detail the pattern of function and operation intended by the Lord for His body, the church. When the church understands its roots and follows its pattern, the servant-people will fulfill its mission with God's fullest blessing.

The revelation concerning the church

The inspired writers of the Bible sought to give a comprehensive view. They looked back, around, and forward. The four Gospels and Acts tell what happened historically. The twenty-one Epistles, which vary in length, treat practical and doctrinal issues that arose in the churches as they then existed. The Revelation prophesied of days to come.

While the early church always recognized its historical basis, it never sought a static existence, nor did it recognize itself as cast into a permanent mold. Changes demanded adjustment, and, with flexibility, the Christians fitted principle to need. When the day arrived that the apostolic leaders were pressed into duties that blunted their ministry of the Word and prayer, the office of deacon was devised. When the synagogues no longer were suitable for the advancement of the gospel, private homes were used.

Experimental ventures of the first Christian church included communal living. When the church at Antioch felt incapable of settling certain doctrinal issues, the church at Jerusalem was approached by its delegates and assembled for its counsel. Churches were harassed by factors of their environment and perplexed by problems of life and organization, but always there was the creative response born of the Holy Spirit that met the need. In short, it may be said that while using guidance from history and God's revelation, the church sought relevance always by applying changeless truth to changing times.

God's revelation of redemption is still the church's authority. Christ founded the church (Eph. 2:20) and gave it His Word that it might become *God's household . . . the pillar and foundation of the truth* (1 Tim. 3:15). The church of the New Testament in its development is our pattern.

The development of the church

The early church grew rapidly. After Peter preached on the

23

day of Pentecost three thousand souls were saved. The new Christians *accepted his message, were baptized* in obedience to the Great Commission of Matthew 28:19, and *devoted themselves to the apostles' teaching and to the fellowship, to the breaking of bread and to prayer* (Acts 2:41-42). Later, five thousand men were saved (Acts 4:4) and the number *increased rapidly, and a large number of priests became obedient to the faith* (Acts 6:7).

It is estimated by church historians that at the time of Stephen's death at least twenty-five thousand had been added to the Christian church and at the close of the first century, five hundred thousand. Acts 8 reveals the extension of the church to Samaria, and with the conversion of Paul there soon followed the missionary journeys from Antioch by which the Christian church was extended to the entire known world over which Rome ruled.

The direction of the church

The pastoral Epistles of First and Second Timothy and Titus are highly significant for their revelation of the time when the church took on definite organizational form. The need of wholesome teaching had arisen which would sift out disbeliefs and test the practicality and fullness of the truth. Regulations of public worship, qualifications for pastors and deacons, administration of the church, and matters of doctrine and sober practice occupy these epistles.

The New Testament assumes that the world will always consciously or unconsciously judge what the church says by what it is. The church's power and effectiveness rest largely with its character.

Christ through the apostles left behind a servant-people, a fellowship that is an explicit provision for the extension of His saving power to the whole world. These servant-people are called, trained, endowed, and sent forth to fulfill the Great Commission.

2

The Church in Its Spiritual Nature

Christianity is primarily the Spirit and power of Christ, represented in the world by believers and expressed through the local church. This representation is sometimes called the "mystical body of Christ," but it refers specifically to those who have been united spiritually to Christ (Col. 2:2), are born again, and have a sincere love for other believers (Eph. 4:2-6; 1 Pet. 1:22-23).

A church is more than a building or a membership. Actually, these are incidental to the primary aspect, which is the invisible and spiritual. The church as a local body of people who worship, bear testimony, serve, and support the preaching and teaching of God's Word has failings and virtues just as Israel had in the Old Testament.

In the measure in which the church represents the true body of Christ spiritually, it is comprised of all believers of all ages, including those who have gone on before and who are *spirits of righteous men made perfect* in heaven (Heb. 12:23). All of these are justified saints because they came *to Jesus the mediator of a new covenant, and to the sprinkled blood that speaks a better word than the blood of Abel* (Heb. 12:24).

This spiritual aspect must be thoroughly understood if the physical aspect, such as The Christian and Missionary Alliance organization, is to have meaning and direction.

Christ's own relationship to the church spiritually must be considered because the church is the body of Christ on earth.

Christ, the Head of the Body

The transition from the Old Testament to the New Testament did not come easy. Many of the New Testament Epistles were written to explain how Christ's fulfillment of the Old Testament had created a new dimension for living to serve God. The old priesthood, sacrifices, religious festivals, and the Sabbath were to be understood in terms of what Jesus Christ had accomplished.

Those who persisted in perverting the messianic significance of Christ had to be confronted. The Colossian believers who were influenced by Judaistic teaching thus were challenged by the Apostle Paul:

> *Just as you received Christ Jesus as Lord, continue to live in him, rooted and built up in him, strengthened in the faith as you were taught, and overflowing with thankfulness.*
>
> *See to it that no one takes you captive through hollow and deceptive philosophy, which depends on human tradition . . . what you eat or drink, or with regard to a religious festival, a New Moon celebration or a Sabbath day. These are a shadow of the things that were to come; the reality, however, is found in Christ. ₁The man with the unspiritual mind₁ has lost connection with the Head, from whom the whole body, supported and held together by its ligaments and sinews, grows as God causes it to grow* (Col. 2:6-8, 16-17, 19).

Christ, the founder of the church

The disciples represented a nucleus in Israel who accepted Christ's proclamation of the kingdom of God that was at hand. At Caesarea Philippi, when He announced to them His purpose to build His church, Peter confessed that Jesus was truly the Messiah (Matt. 16:16-18). Jesus and His disciples did not form a separate synagogue or temple, but an open fellowship within Israel whose only identity was that they followed Jesus.

After Jesus Christ's death and Resurrection 120 disciples directly followed Jesus. They were instructed by Jesus to wait on God until the Holy Spirit would be outpoured upon them. They waited forty days during which time Jesus appeared to them from time to time to instruct them regarding the kingdom of God (Acts 1:3).

The disciples had presupposed that the kingdom would be a theocratic kingdom of Jews on earth, but Jesus indicated He had another priority—the outpouring of the Holy Spirit as promised by John the Baptist (Matt. 3:11). The disciples had asked, *"Lord, are you at this time going to restore the kingdom to Israel?"* Jesus had answered:

"It is not for you to know the times or dates the Father has set by his own authority. But you will receive power when the Holy Spirit comes on you; and you will be my witnesses in Jerusalem, and in all Judea and Samaria, and to the ends of the earth" (Acts 1:6-8).

Just what this would mean in terms of lifestyle for a New Testament body of believers could be disclosed only as the opportunity for reflection arose from the teaching of the Holy Spirit.

John the Baptist prophesied that Jesus would be the One to effect the baptism of the Holy Spirit (Mark 1:8). On the day of Pentecost, the Jewish festival when the first harvest grain was presented to God in thanksgiving, the Holy Spirit was outpoured. Several phenomena occurred with symbolic significance.

Suddenly a sound like the blowing of a violent wind came from heaven and filled the whole house where they were sitting (Acts 2:2). This wind signified the indisputable and pervading presence of the Holy Spirit. Jesus spoke of this when He discussed with Nicodemus the need to be born again (John 3:5-8).

Further, *they saw what seemed to be tongues of fire that separated and came to rest on each of them* (Acts 2:3). This bore a distinct likeness to the pillar of fire that led Israel through the Red Sea and in the wilderness and had rested upon the Holy of Holies when the tabernacle was set up in the midst of Israel's camp. The disciples knew that the spiritual veil had been torn as the temple veil was torn in two

27

when Jesus Christ died (Luke 23:45). Every believer at Pentecost became a priest in union with the risen, exalted Christ to whom all power had been given.

A third phenomenon occurred: *All of them were filled with the Holy Spirit and began to speak in other tongues as the Spirit enabled them* (Acts 2:4). This was an extension of Joel's prophecy that God would pour out His Spirit upon all His people (Joel 2:28-29), not only upon the appointed kings, priests, and prophets as in the Old Tesament. This signified that the gospel was for all people universally as in sixteen named foreign languages people understood the praises of the 120 in their own tongue (Acts 2:8-11). This phenomenon occurred again at the house of a Roman centurion (Acts 10) and at Ephesus upon some Greeks who had not yet heard that Jesus had risen and had been exalted to send the Holy Spirit (Acts 19).

These phenomena were given to convince the disciples and others who believed the gospel that the full transition had come. Thus, the baptism John had promised had now occurred to form the church Jesus had promised.

Christ, the fulfillment of the promises

Christ, the Suffering Servant of the book of Isaiah, since Pentecost has been represented in a body of people called "the church." When the 120 disciples experienced the pentecostal gift, Peter interpreted this as the last days having arrived: *This is what was spoken by the prophet Joel: "In the last days, God says, I will pour out my Spirit on all people.... And everyone who calls on the name of the Lord will be saved"* (Acts 2:16-17, 21).

The many God-fearing Jews who had gathered at Jerusalem for the feast of Pentecost and who were attracted by the sound of a mighty wind and the witnessing of the 120 in various languages, responded to Peter's preaching. They asked, *"Brothers, what shall we do?"* Peter instructed them to believe and be baptized and promised that they, too, would receive the gift of the Holy Spirit. As a result, *those who accepted his message were baptized, and about three thousand were added to their number that day* (Acts 2:37-38, 41). It is significant that these God-fearing Jews undoubtedly had been prepared in seeking the consolation of Israel, even as had Anna and Simeon (Luke 2:25-38).

Pentecost marked a transition by adding in oneness those who believed and were baptized. The significance of this was explained to believers of the church at Corinth: *For we were all baptized by one Spirit into one body—whether Jews or Greeks, slave or free—and we were all given the one Spirit to drink* (1 Cor. 12:13).

Christ, the authority of the church

After His Resurrection Jesus declared to His disciples: *"All authority in heaven and on earth has been given to me. Therefore go and make disciples of all nations, baptizing them in the name of the Father and of the Son and of the Holy Spirit, and teaching them to obey everything I have commanded you. And surely I will be with you always, to the very end of the age"* (Matt. 28:18-20).

Again, when He appeared to His disciples and ate with them, He said:

"This is what I told you while I was still with you: Everything must be fulfilled that is written about me in the Law of Moses, the Prophets and the Psalms."

Then he opened their minds so they could understand the Scriptures. He told them, "This is what is written: The Christ will suffer and rise from the dead on the third day, and repentance and forgiveness of sins will be preached in his name to all nations, beginning at Jerusalem" (Luke 24:44-47).

The Christ who is to be known and believed in is the Christ of the Scriptures; the only spirit that can make Christ known is the Holy Spirit. The Spirit and the Bible, and the Bible and Christ form an inseparable mosaic of divine authority. Included in the Great Commission is the charge to bring all new disciples under the authority of the word of Christ (Matt. 28:20).

The writers of the New Testament occupied a crucial position in the plan of Redemption and in the founding of the church. They witnessed to the life, teaching, death, and Resurrection of Jesus Christ and were inspired by the Holy Spirit to produce the New Testament which was binding on the church.

Believers, the Members of His Body

According to Ephesians 4:12, the work of the ministry is not the responsibility of paid professionals, but is the job of every believer who represents God's servant-people. Those in leadership ministry are *to prepare God's people for works of service, so that the body of Christ may be built up.*

Because the work of the ministry is a spiritual work, God provides His church with spiritual enablement to carry it out. God has a design in the church and a provision for it that needs to be understood.

Members of Christ

The church is first an organism—a living body of people who are different members of the same body—the body of Christ. Having been baptized by one Spirit into one body, it is impossible for a person to be a believer and not to be in the church spiritually. This is not all that matters in regard to a believer's relationship to the church, but it is the most important.

Churches are prone to entrust the work of the ministry to people who exhibit natural ability. They, however, will fail miserably if they have no appreciation for the body of Christ spiritually and if they lack spiritual enablement that is needed to serve in the body of Christ.

Before Jesus was led to the cross He prayed a long prayer of intercession that revealed His concern for the disciples of the future. It is often called the "high-priestly prayer" of Jesus (John 17). In praying for all future believers, He was concerned about their unity:

"My prayer is not for them alone₍his twelve disciples₎. I pray also for those who will believe in me through their message, that all of them may be one, Father, just as you are in me and I am in you. May they also be in us so that the world may believe that you have sent me. I have given them the glory that you gave me, that they may be one as we are one: I in them and you in me. May they be brought to complete unity to let the

world know that you sent me and have loved them even as you have loved me" (John 17:20-23).

For Christ to manifest Himself to the world through believers so that the world will believe required that they be one organism. The Holy Spirit's function is to form a composite of believers who together are able to manifest Christ and His work more fully than is possible by isolated individualism. Humans, in general, may look for a superman, but God is interested in churches where there are people who find unity in Christ by the way they relate to one another.

The prophets spoke of this unity: *How good and pleasant it is when brothers live together in unity!* (Ps. 133:1) They prophesied of another day when God's people would be united under the ministry of God's Word: *Listen! Your watchmen lift up their voices; together they shout for joy. When the* LORD *returns to Zion, they will see it with their own eyes* (Isa. 52:8).

The apostles admonished the churches:

May the God who gives endurance and encouragement give you a spirit of unity among yourselves as you follow Christ Jesus, so that with one heart and mouth you may glorify the God and Father of our Lord Jesus Christ.

Accept one another, then, just as Christ accepted you, in order to bring praise to God (Rom. 15:5-7).

I appeal to you, brothers, in the name of our Lord Jesus Christ, that all of you agree with one another so that there may be no divisions among you and that you may be perfectly united in mind and thought (1 Cor. 1:10).

Because Christ is to be manifested through their oneness, unity among God's people has deep spiritual significance to the life of the church and in its outreach to the world.

Members one of another

One of the most significant elements of an early description of the church is its sense of fellowship: *They devoted themselves to the apostles' teaching and to the fellowship* (Acts 2:42). The quality of this oneness (Acts 2:44, 47) was a result of their unity in Christ. To be a believer meant to share with other believers the sense of being free from sin, loved by Christ, and sent as witnesses to the world. They had a sense of common resourcefulness in each other's spiritual gifts. The Spirit of Christ that they held in common made them care deeply for each other.

The Apostle Paul drew analogy from the human body:

Now the body is not made up of one part but of many.

The eye cannot say to the hand, "I don't need you!"

And the head cannot say to the feet, "I don't need you!"

If one part suffers, every part suffers with it; if one part is honored, every part rejoices with it (1 Cor. 12:14, 21, 26).

A believer is meant to share with other believers and never to live in isolation. God placed believers in the body with a capacity to render worshipful service.

In the Bible the union of Christ and the church is illustrated by the union of husband and wife (Eph. 5). A church can give birth and nurture to healthy spiritual children only as it maintains a warm spirit of vital fellowship. Dr. A.B. Simpson, the founder of The Christian and Missionary Alliance, wrote that

we must . . . maintain a healthful spiritual condition, or we shall defile the whole body by sympathetic contact. And, therefore, if we are filled with the Spirit, we shall have a very tender, compassionate and sympathetic heart toward Christ's church, and shall be solicitous and sensitive for her welfare and prosperity. It will be our joy, like the great apostle's, "to be offered upon the sacrifice and services of her faith," and to "fill up that which remains of the sufferings of Christ for His body, the Church"; sharing with the blessed Head the needs of His people, bearing one another burdens, and so fulfilling the law of Christ (*Power from on High*, Vol. 2, p. 122).

Members of mutual purpose

As members of Christ and His fellowship, we who make up the church have both a local and a universal purpose. The disciples were told to wait for the promise of the Father until the Holy Spirit would come, and they were to become God's witnesses *in Jerusalem, and in all Judea and Samaria, and to the ends of the earth* (Acts 1:18).

The book of Acts depicts God's design in the church as fulfilling Jesus' Great Commission and describes how a small fellowship of believers in Jerusalem became represented by a racially mixed fellowship in the capital city of Rome. It was a switch from Israel and its nationalism to a cosmopolitan church with a worldwide outreach.

The spiritual nature of the church depends largely on its view of Christ as universal sovereign. Christ's ascension and enthronement, accompanied by the coming of the Holy Spirit, are explained to us on a personal basis:

But to each one of us grace has been given as Christ apportioned it. This is why it says:

'When he ascended on high,
he led captives in his train
and gave gifts to men.'

(What does 'he ascended' mean except that he also descended to the lower, earthly regions? He who descended is the very one who ascended higher than all the heavens, in order to fill the whole universe.) It was he who gave some to be apostles, some to be prophets, some to be evangelists, and some to be pastors and teachers, to prepare God's people for works of service, so that the body of Christ may be built up (Eph. 4:7-12).

Each of us, then, is to be part of Christ's great universal purpose because He is a universal sovereign. Therefore, Paul prayed for the Ephesian believers:

I pray also that the eyes of your heart may be enlightened in order that you may know the hope to which he has called you, the riches of his glorious inheritance in the saints, and his incomparably great power for us who believe. That power is like the working of his mighty strength, which he exerted in Christ when he raised him from the dead and seated him at his right hand in the heavenly realms, far above all rule and authority, power and dominion, and every title that can be given, not only in the present age but also in the one to come. And God placed all things under his feet and appointed him to be head over everything for the church, which is his body, the fullness of him who fills everything in every way (Eph. 1:18-23).

Each member of the church should put needs and problems in proper priority. Jesus exhorted:

So do not worry, saying, 'What shall we eat?' or 'What shall we drink?' or 'What shall we wear?' For the pagans run after all these things, and your heavenly Father knows that you need them. But seek first his kingdom and his righteousness, and all these things will be given to you as well (Matt. 6:31-33).

The spiritual nature of the church is not some empty idealism that is impractical for daily living. Rather, it is a realism that includes what we eat, drink, and wear. To have our value system established according to God's plan is to be assured that everything we need will be provided.

Members having gifts for service
Each one should use whatever gift he has received to serve others, faithfully administering God's grace in its various forms (1 Pet. 4:10).

The Holy Spirit sovereignly provides supernatural gifts to believers so that the church will be better equipped to fulfill its mission. These gifts are important and are given for the good of the whole church.

The composite that God creates through believers' various gifts gives the church a versatile, effective ministry. Through the unity of believers in local churches Christ is made real as people of different backgrounds, financial resources, intellectual capacities, ages, or sex are dedicated to the service of Christ (John 17:23).

Christ, as head of the church, equips His people and sets their gifts in the body life of the church in such a way that members may serve each other and be used in such a relationship to reach a lost world (Eph. 4:12-16). Like natural abilities, spiritual gifts fit the personality of the believer and the propriety of the occasion whenever and wherever such ministries are needed.

While some gifts are quite different from natural abilities, such as miracles, healings, tongues, and interpretation of tongues, others are similar. These latter gifts include administration, ruling, helping, showing mercy, and the word of wisdom. Others, such as the gifts of those called to be apostles, pastor-teachers, and elder-bishops, reveal a particular blend of endowment with natural ability that God sanctifies for official leadership.

The Corinthians lacked no spiritual gift (1 Cor. 1:7) and yet were worldly and unspiritual (1 Cor. 3:3), partly because they flaunted certain gifts as proving superlative evidence of the Spirit (1 Cor. 12—13). The Corinthians were instructed that all the gifts were for the edifying or building up of the body and that a humble servant attitude ruled by love was the highest attainment of all.

Much of the explanation for the differences that exist widely in the church today is that Christians tend to look at things that are seen instead of the things that are unseen (2 Cor. 4:18). As we look at problems in the church and alongside it a suffering world beset by bigotry and hatred, the obvious solution seems to be to marshal all our human resources to meet those problems and needs. Such thinking is shallow and superficial and treats symptoms, not causes.

Basic to a realistic understanding of the church is its spiritual nature, and in this spiritual nature the ultimate answers lie.

3

The Church and Its Visible Nature

Although the spiritual nature of the church supersedes the visible, both are necessary. God has ordained that the spiritual should be made manifest, even as *the fullness of the Deity lives in bodily form* (Col. 2:9).

Our spiritual redemption was accomplished through Christ's physical death. *He himself bore our sins in his body on the tree* (1 Pet. 2:24). The physical Resurrection of Christ represents the hope of our physical resurrection; our future transformed bodies shall be like His glorious body manifested during the forty days after the Resurrection (Phil. 3:21).

The Greek word *ekklesia* is used 115 times in the New Testament. In 90 of these references it is used to describe specific local congregations, whereas at other times it is used to refer to the mystical or spiritual body of Christ.

Paul uses both spiritual and visible in writing to the Corinthians: *Now you are the body of Christ, and each one of you is a part of it* (1 Cor. 12:27). If Paul had been speaking only of the church spiritually, he would have included himself.

In another Scripture, Paul includes himself and then excludes himself: *For we are God's fellow workers; you are God's field, God's building* (1 Cor. 3:9). From the context we learn that Apollos, Peter, and Paul had at various times ministered to establish the Corinthian church. Those, however, who remained in that specific locality represented, as it were, a cultivated field or a building in which an enterprising business was conducted.

The Equipment of the Church

Any reference to a visible church usually causes one to think of a building. Today, churches have buildings, but this was not the general rule for the first 400 years of the church.

Actually, the visible characteristics of the church are other than a building. The important visible features of the church are God-ordained and need to be recognized and understood by all.

The Bible
God has expressed His authority by a written revelation. The church and the Bible go together and are necessary to each other. How central and significant the actual words of Scripture were to be is recognized by the words of Jesus Christ to His disciples after the Resurrection:

"This is what I told you while I was still with you: Everything must be fulfilled that is written about me in the Law of Moses, the Prophets and the Psalms."

Then he opened their minds so they could understand the Scriptures. He told them, "This is what is written: The Christ will suffer and rise from the dead on the third day, and repentance and forgiveness of sins will be preached in his name to all nations, beginning at Jerusalem" (Luke 24:44-47).

Jesus used the Old Testament as a body of truth that declared Him to be Lord (John 5:37-40). When He began His ministry He went to the synagogue, where He had attended faithfully as a boy, opened the Scriptures to Isaiah 61:1-2, and declared that Scripture was fulfilled even as the hearers listened (Luke 4:16-21).

The early church followed the example Jesus set regarding the Scriptures. The Apostle Paul spoke of the church as being built upon the foundation of the apostles and prophets and that Jesus Christ himself was its chief cornerstone (Eph. 2:20).

Apostolic tradition and teaching, when completed and collated, received the same recognition of authority as the Old Testament. These were designated to be read before early church congregations and were exchanged among the churches (Col. 4:16; 1 Thess. 5:27; Rev. 1:3) to be received as the Word of God (1 Cor. 11:23; 1 Thess. 2:13).

The importance of the Word of God to the church is reflected in Paul's instruction to Timothy, who was pastor at Ephesus:

Although I hope to come to you soon, I am writing you these instructions so that, if I am delayed, you will know how people ought to conduct themselves in God's household, which is the church of the living God, the pillar and foundation of the truth (1 Tim. 3:14-15).

The church is so identified with the Bible and the Christ it proclaims that it can understand itself in terms of the Bible's declaration.

The proclamation of the Word

The Bible teaches that when Christ ascended He *gave some to be apostles, some to be prophets, some to be evangelists, and some to be pastors and teachers, to prepare God's people for works of service, so that the body of Christ may be built up* (Eph. 4:11-12). Those appointed to proclaim God's Word and give oversight to its functions are to be shepherds of God's flock by both their example and their preaching (1 Pet. 5:2-4). God speaks through the preacher so that what is true to God's Word will emerge in the life of the church as a body.

Paul commended the Thessalonian church because they received his preaching not as the word of men, but as the Word of God, which works in those who believe. This was true also of God's churches in Judea (1 Thess. 2:13-14).

The church is to believe that God himself is present and actively speaking His Word in the pulpit proclamation of the church when a man called of God preaches the Word. The written form of the Word is to find significant expression through human personality in much the same pattern as the Word which was made flesh in Jesus Christ fulfilled the written Word. When God's people make an appointment with

God in God's house and God's Word is preached by God-sent men, His Word will unite God's people and accomplish what God intended.

The ordinances

Another external or visible equipment of the church is referred to as "ordinances." Four Greek words translated *ordinances* in the King James Version of the Bible are translated variously in other versions (cf. 1 Cor. 11:2; Heb. 9:1, 10; 1 Pet. 2:13).

Basically, an ordinance is that which has been appointed by the Lord. Even though *ordinance* is not applied to baptism or to the Lord's Supper in the Bible, nevertheless it is clear that these have been appointed for special observance, and thus they have been called ordinances of the church.

Jesus included baptism in the Great Commission. At the Passover feast before His Crucifixion, He instituted the Lord's Supper. The Apostle Paul claims by direct revelation the observance and function of the Lord's Supper (1 Cor. 11:23 ff.).

Everywhere in the book of Acts where people are said to have believed, they were baptized also. Preaching and the breaking of bread, or the Lord's table, were part of their regular observance on the first day of the week (Acts 20:7; cf. 1 Cor. 16:2). These two ordinances serve to symbolize two great truths of the gospel—Christ's atoning death and victorious Resurrection.

Baptism. The external rite of baptism symbolized the salvation experience of the early believers in that spiritually they had come to the cross to be identified with Christ in His death and Resurrection. They had believed and now were confessing their conversion experience by baptism.

On the day of Pentecost, Peter exhorted every one of the hearers to repent and be baptized in the name of Jesus Christ (Acts 2:38). Repentance and conversion mean "to turn," "to turn about face," or "to believe with a whole heart." In the accounts in the book of Acts, only those who were already believers were baptized: *When they believed . . . they were baptized, both men and women* (Acts 8:12).

On one occasion a man who had been a sorcerer professed

to believe and was baptized; but later Peter perceived that he was still in need of repentance and was *full of bitterness and captive to sin* (Acts 8:21-23).

Paul obviously was relieved that at Corinth he had baptized very few of the professing converts (1 Cor. 1:14) because of their failure to reflect true conversion to the Lord and because they were so enamored of human ministers.

By baptism the convert declares that he wants to be counted in all that is necessary to discipleship with a profession that is unashamed and open for all to see. He has openly come from the world and committed himself to Christ and to His service, cutting every tie that would bind him.

The meaning and symbol are associated closely. The word *baptize* (Greek *baptisma*) means "to immerse," and by baptism death is symbolized by going down under the water and resurrection to newness of life by coming up out of the water (Rom. 6:1-7). The accounts in the book of Acts and the earliest historical records attest to this practice. Thus, believers were identified as in the body of Christ.

The Lord's Supper. God also has made provision by which fellowship in the gospel is to be expressed in a representative company of believers through the ordinance of Communion (Matt. 26:26-29; Mark 14:22-26; Luke 22:14-20; 1 Cor. 11:23-26). He said, *"Do this in remembrance of me."* Jesus inaugurated His own memorial as it was to be observed by His own disciples. It marked visibly the provision that had been made by which fellowship was to be expressed in Communion.

The partaking of the elements, the bread and the wine, again proclaim the centrality of Christ's work on the cross and the provision of His Atonement. All strained relationships between members are to be put away, and an examination of relationship to Christ and to fellow believers is to precede the holy ordinance (John 13:13-20; 1 Cor. 11:27-31).

The corporate character of a church will be the result of the various personalities that compose the body. The perspective in which the internal life and order are to be kept and the efficiency in which all will work to a purposeful end will be determined ultimately by the character of individual members. While the church is first an organism brought to life by the Spirit of Christ, its organization safeguards the organism and defines its task. The invisible fellowship should be marked visibly by Communion.

The ordinances of baptism and Communion are intended to declare the initial identification of the believer and the continuing fellowship of the believing ones. Both are to be observed until Jesus comes again (Matt. 28:20; 1 Cor. 11:26). They identify the physical church in a particular way. Baptism, symbolizing the new birth, is observed but once by the believer while the Lord's Supper is repeated often, signifying that one's spiritual life is maintained and strengthened by continued fellowship with Christ and with those who share that life in Christ.

The gifts and callings of the members

Gifts and callings in the church are to be recognized with intelligence (1 Cor. 12:1). Although His gifts are spiritual, God wants to provide enablings, skills, energizings, and directions that are so blended in the physical organization and operation of the church that Christ's own life and ministry will be made real through His people.

Without members called by God and gifted by the Holy Spirit the physical church could not exist. Neither the organization nor the clergy constitutes the church, but all the members who corporately hold their gifts and callings in common for the purpose of ministering. The church is basically a dynamic organism with a function to perform and is made up of a new servant-people "called out" (English word *church* is the Greek word *ekklesia*, meaning "to call out") to do business for Jesus Christ. He drew this analogy in a parable:

> *It's like a man going away: He leaves his house in charge of his servants, each with his assigned task, and tells the one at the door to keep watch.*
>
> *Therefore keep watch because you do not know when the owner of the house will come back. . . . If he comes suddenly, do not let him find you sleeping* (Mark 13: 34-36).

The Leadership of the Church

Primarily, the church is a body designed to express through each individual member the life of Christ and is equipped by the Holy Spirit with gifts designed to manifest Christ corporately. Certain gifts are provided to give leadership to the church, and, while every Christian is to minister, the work of the leaders is to equip them to minister in order to build up the body of Christ (Eph. 4:11-12).

"Building up the body" involves bringing men and women who do not have a personal relationship to Jesus Christ into fellowship with Him and into responsible church membership and to bring all believers to maturity. This is the responsibility of local church leaders whom the New Testament calls *elders* and *deacons*.

The office of elder

The Bible designates two classes of elders, those who both teach and direct the church's affairs and those who direct the affairs but do not ordinarily preach and teach:

> *The elders who direct the affairs of the church well are worthy of double honor, especially those whose work is preaching and teaching* (1 Tim. 5:17).

The origin of the office of elder in the New Testament church is not recorded, but elders existed almost from the beginning of the church (Acts 11:30). In the book of Acts are references also to *elders of Israel* (Acts 4:5, 8, 23; 6:12; 23:14; 24:1; 25:15).

Lay elders. The office of elder began with a special function when the administrative load of Moses became too heavy and the Lord provided relief:

> *"Bring me seventy of Israel's elders who are known to you as leaders and officials among the people. Have them come to the Tent of Meeting, that they may stand there with you. I will come down and speak with you there, and I will take of the Spirit that is on you and put the Spirit on them. They will help you carry the burden of the people so that you will not have to carry it alone"* (Num. 11:16-17).

It was the heritage of this office that continued in the period of the judges, throughout the period of the monarchy, during the captivity, and after return from captivity. A council of elders presided over the affairs of every Jewish synagogue. The Christians at first worshiped in the synagogue until they were forced to form house churches because of persecution from the Jews.

After the church was established in Jerusalem and in other parts of the world, the same term was used to refer to the elders of the church (Acts 14:23; 15:2, 4, 6, 22-23; 16:4; 20:17; 21:18). Three passages make reference to both elders and overseers (bishops): 1 Timothy 3:1-7; Titus 1:5-9, and 1 Peter 5:1-5. Although the offices of elders and overseers are used interchangeably, there seems to be a distinction between those who gave oversight to the affairs of the church and those who gave oversight and also preached and taught the Word.

Certain responsibilities rest upon elders generally. They should pray and care for the entire membership, respond to requests to pray for and anoint the sick, and with the pastor, the chief elder, oversee and shepherd the flock. Multiple eldership is God's divine plan to make possible, even in the largest church, a people-centered ministry of pastoral care.

Whenever Paul had guided the establishment of a church in his missionary journeys, he commissioned elders:

Paul and Barnabas appointed elders for them in each church and, with prayer and fasting, committed them to the Lord in whom they had put their trust (Acts 14:23).

Preaching and teaching elders. First Peter 5:2 divides the responsibilities of these elders into two classes: shepherding God's flock and overseeing (cf. Acts 20:28; 2 Tim. 4:5). Shepherding is to preach and teach the Word. Along with this, the shepherd or pastor, as head elder, is to render oversight. Without the officiating proclamation of the Word in the church, the oversight would be pointless.

To be sure, pastors also serve with noble purpose as counselors and administrators. They often comfort the sick and the dying, but it is still the proclamation of God's Word that the world needs. Only as the church obeys the word of proclamation will it notably affect the world.

Time and again Israel was reminded that they had been called into existence by the Word of God, much as the first chapter of Genesis depicts the world as framed by the Word of God (cf. Isa. 43:1; 44:2, 21-24; 49:1, 5, 15; 51:1-2; John 1:1-3; Heb. 1:1-2). But Paul states explicitly:

But not all the Israelites accepted the good news. For Isaiah says, "Lord, who has believed our message?" Consequently, faith comes from hearing the message, and the message is heard through the word of Christ (Rom. 10:16-17).

What applied to Israel now applies to the church, for in the context Paul refers to both Jew and Gentile and asks:

How, then, can they call on the one they have not believed in? And how can they believe in the one of whom they have not heard? And how can they hear without someone preaching to them? And how can they preach unless they are sent? (Rom. 10:14-15).

It is no wonder, then, that the emphasis upon the work of the pastor, or bishop-elder, is his preaching and teaching.

Like Jesus, the elders are to reveal God's Word in words and in deeds. The Word is to take form in works and the church is to represent both. Therefore, the pastor cannot relinquish oversight even though elders help to carry the load.

Timothy ministered as a pastor and prophesied (1 Tim. 4:14), but he was commanded also to teach (1 Tim. 4:11; 6:2; 2 Tim. 2:2), to *preach the Word; be prepared in season and out of season; correct, rebuke and encourage—with great patience and careful instruction* (2 Tim. 4:2).

The office of deacons and deaconesses

In Philippians 1:1 and 1 Timothy 3:8-10, the offices of elder and deacon are described as common in the early church. The Timothy passage sets forth specific qualifications for deacons that are comparable to that of the elders.

The word *deacon* is a transliteration in the English from the Greek and means simply "servant." In Greek culture there were servants in the household who were slaves. In Christian culture the word *servant* had a noble connotation that was associated directly with Jesus Christ. Paul called himself *a slave of Jesus Christ* when he used a most coveted title, and he used it often.

In a growing church at Jerusalem in its beginning stages the institution of the office of deacon met a definite need. Evidently, the widows of the Hebrews were favored above those of the Greeks who needed special help. The neglect developed because the apostles were overloaded with the care and oversight of the church.

Deacons. The office of deacon was suggested by the apostles and instituted by the combined authority of the apostles and of the entire church for a particular reason, as expressed by the Twelve to the other disciples:

> *"It would not be right for us to neglect the ministry of the word of God in order to wait on tables. Brothers, choose seven men from among you who are known to be full of the Spirit and wisdom. We will turn this responsibility over to them and will give our attention to prayer and the ministry of the word"* (Acts 6:2-4).

The most significant aspect of the office was to cover those areas of ministry that would allow the apostles or the elders to concentrate on the ministry of the Word. It was not that the work of the deacons was material and the work of the elders spiritual, but simply that the priorities might have proper attention. Deacons like Philip and Stephen witnessed and ministered the Word to the unsaved, but even then their ministry was complementary to that of the apostles.

Because of this supportive role, deacons serve to maintain oversight of church property, church finances and legal documents, the benevolences, and any special ministries of evangelism and visitation as necessities arise and as their gifts fit the need.

Deaconesses. In the early church also were women who were deaconesses with a regular responsibility of service in the church. It seems probable, from implication in the New Testament, that the wives of elders and of deacons were considered as part of the offices their husbands occupied (Rom. 16:3).

Widows and single women who were free to serve without

restrictive responsibilities at home are noted especially as deaconesses in the New Testament. The widows who, in co-operation with their husbands, had served faithfully were to be supported by the church (1 Tim. 5:9-10).

The gifts of apostles, prophets, and evangelists

Evidently there were gifts related to churches at large. Ephesians 4:11 speaks of Christ's having given *some to be apostles, some to be prophets, some to be evangelists* who serve the church uniquely. The function of these is not described as explicitly as that of elders and deacons, but their mention in Ephesians and their description in the New Testament elsewhere relates their ministry as not confined to a local church but to churches at large.

Apostles. There are those who believe that the office of apostle could not be repeated or transmitted because of Peter's restriction. Judas's successor was to be someone who had been with the twelve apostles the whole time Jesus was with them and who had witnessed Jesus' Resurrection (Acts 1:21-22). Matthias, who was chosen on the particular occasion when Peter spoke, is not mentioned again in the New Testament record.

Paul considered himself an apostle, and as one who had seen the Lord (1 Cor. 9:1), yet he did not meet Peter's qualifications. He was not with Jesus during His earthly ministry, nor was he a witness of the Lord's Resurrection during the forty days, though the Lord had appeared to him as one *abnormally born* (1 Cor. 15:8).

Direct witness from the Lord as revelation bearers was no doubt the qualification of those whose ministry and writing established the early church (Eph. 2:20). Such are not repeated as gifts. But in general it meant simply "one sent forth," a messenger, particularly as an ambassador. When Paul speaks of the gifts given to the church profusely and in variety he asks, *Are all apostles? Are all prophets? Are all teachers?* (1 Cor. 12:29) and leaves the clear implication that these were continuing gifts.

There were apostles in the early church who met neither Paul's nor Peter's qualifications of having seen the Lord either during His ministry or by direct appearance (Acts 14:4, 14; Rom. 16:7; Gal. 1:19; 2:9).

The Latin word for *apostle, missionar,* means "one commissioned with a definite mission and responsible to the sender as an ambassador." From this we get the familiar term *missionaries.* They are sent out by the church to found and establish churches in cross-cultural situations and form a significant role in fulfilling the Great Commission.

The first examples of this, as described in Acts 13:1-3, were Paul and Barnabas. Not only were they sent out by the church, but they reported back to the churches who had sent them (Acts 14:26-28). Not all will agree that Hudson Taylor should be called "Apostle to China" or Adoniram Judson "Apostle to Burma," but we use the word *missionary* to identify a ministry of the church, though it does not appear in the New Testament.

Prophets. The prophets associated with the apostles in establishing the New Testament in Ephesians 2:20 refer to those of the Old Testament record who spoke by direct witness from God and formed important revelational background for Christ's coming. But, again, as noted with the apostles, the classification can be too restricted.

The gift of prophecy did not end with the Old Testament and is recognized in the New Testament as a continuing gift (1 Cor. 12:29). Prophets ministered to the churches the *mystery of Christ* (Eph. 3:4-5), resided in certain localities, or ministered in an itinerant fashion as the need arose (Acts 11:27; 13:1; 15:32; 1 Tim. 1:18; 4:14).

Deacons, apostles, and pastors or elders possessed various spiritual gifts and served at times as prophets, evangelists, and teachers, but there were those whose gift to edify the church carried the significance of a prophet in particular. Today we usually call them "revivalists" who minister in church renewal, and, like the Old Testament prophets, they bring a new sense of direction to God's people.

Evangelists. The word *evangelist* means simply "one who announces the good news." The major example of this was Philip who *preached the good news of the kingdom of God and the name of Jesus Christ* (Acts 8:12). When Paul returned from his third missionary journey he *stayed at the house of Philip the evangelist* (Acts 21:8). From being a deacon and an evangelist Philip evidently developed a distinct vocation as an evangelist only.

Paul admonished Timothy, a pastor, *Do the work of an evangelist, discharge all the duties of your ministry* (2 Tim. 4:5), but the term *evangelist* is used only three times in the New Testament record. The third is in reference to those gifts given to the church in the preparation of saints for the work of the ministry (Eph. 4:11). This term, however, is familiar to the contemporary church.

The Discipleship in the Church

The visible church must have not only equipment and leadership, but also discipleship. Entrance into Christian discipleship and church membership is a voluntary matter. The acceptance or rejection of someone for membership is a solemn matter, but nevertheless a decision that the church must make.

Regenerated disciples

Safeguards were practiced in the first church to prevent the unregenerate from becoming members. Only those who received Peter's preaching of repentance and faith were baptized and added to the church at Pentecost (Acts 2:41). After God judged Ananias and Sapphira, believers were added, but *no one else dared join them* (Acts 5, esp. vv. 13-14).

Paul admonished the Corinthians to practice judgment in discerning the unregenerate among the believers, reminding them that the unrighteous should not inherit the kingdom of God (1 Cor. 6:1-10). The unrighteous were not to partake of the Lord's Supper because it is impossible to drink of the cup of the Lord and the cup of demons or to partake of the table of the Lord and the table of demons (1 Cor. 10:21).

When Paul came to Ephesus and found certain disciples who did not evidence the regenerating power of the Holy Spirit, he inquired and found that they were baptized with only the baptism of John. He then taught them further to believe on Jesus. These disciples not only believed, but they were baptized again and were filled with the Holy Spirit

(Acts 19:1-7). When Paul continued to preach in this same place, there arose opposition including some who had become obstinate and publicly maligned *the way*. Paul then separated the disciples and departed with them (Acts 19:8-9).

Disciplined disciples

Discipline is required in the membership of the church. Jesus Christ himself gave instruction as to method (Matt. 18:15-18). The context reveals that this is particularly to prevent stumbling of new believers.

A form of ostracism is to be exercised toward those who cause divisions and occasions of stumbling contrary to doctrine (Rom. 16:17). Those who inadvertently fall into sin are to be entreated by those who are spiritual and humble in order to restore them (Gal. 6:1-5). A member guilty of open and serious sin who remains unrepentant is to be dismissed as a wicked person (1 Cor. 5:13). When repentance is manifested he is to be forgiven and comforted *so he will not be overwhelmed by excessive sorrow* (2 Cor. 2:7).

Faithful disciples

True disciples identify themselves with other disciples and remain faithful. John observes

> *They went out from us, but they did not really belong to us. For if they had belonged to us, they would have remained with us; but their going showed that none of them belonged to us* (1 John 2:19).

Christians gathered loyally for many reasons:
- praising God and singing (Acts 2:47; Col. 3:16)
- worship and prayer (Acts 3:1; 4:24; 16:13-14; 18:7)
- the preaching and teaching of the Word (Acts 5:42; 15:35)
- the ministry of edification, exhortation, and comfort (Acts 2:45; 6:1; 1 Cor. 14:3)
- the ministry of evangelism and missions (Acts 13:2-3; Gal. 2:2; Col. 1:29)
- the ministry of giving and labor (Rom. 12:11; 1 Cor. 16:1-3; 1 Thess. 1:3; Heb. 6:10)
- fellowship and service (Eph. 6:7; Phil. 2:30).

Basically, the church is to be a meeting place of faith and works. Busybodies who disrupt the function of the church are to be disciplined (2 Thess. 3:10-12; 1 Tim. 5:11-13; James 2:1-10).

God designed His church with gifted and creative disciples to represent Christ to a needy world. The church is equipped with all that is involved in bringing people into fellowship with Jesus Christ and into responsible church membership. When God's people are faithful there is a balance of form and function in the body of Christ just as there is in a well-developed, healthy human body.

In the visible church practical living in the real world and spiritual mindedness cannot be disjoined. Empty sentimentalism is a disgrace to the church; lack of a sense of direction is a hindrance to the gospel.

Paul admonished the Colossians:

Be wise in your behaviour towards non-Christians, and make the best possible use of your time. Speak pleasantly to them, but never sentimentally, and learn how to give a proper answer to every questioner (Col. 4:5-6, Phillips).

4

The Church As a Functioning Body

The nature of the church governs its function. It has been noted that the church is a spiritual and visible body created for many things, such as worship, training, service, and fellowship. But how is it to function as a growing, meaningful organism to fulfill the complete purpose in God's plan and program?

History abounds in lessons indicating that the main functions of the church often have been taken for granted. Consequently, zeal in some particular aspect of function has led to a serious malformation, as well as malfunction. We dare not attribute these developments to a peculiar providence that has run its course and fulfilled its mission—as though God had "different churches" to fulfill "different missions" for "different times" and permitted future generations to guess what the church ought to be and do. Unless the church has abiding principles to govern its emphases and activities to meet different needs at different times and yet remains true to its mission, its future is without promise.

The Bible, however, is not vague concerning the real function of the church and the principles by which to govern its destiny. While these are not given in fine rules and regulations dated the twentieth century, the pattern is given in terms broad enough, vital enough, and understandable enough to learn to serve God creatively and trustfully and to be led by His Holy Spirit to prove that good, acceptable, and perfect will of God in a world of changing circumstances.

The Nature of the Church's Function

The function of the church has distinctive characteristics that contrast it from Israel of the Old Testament and set it apart from the world to become a self-responsible unit to carry on its ministry.

The church functions as a new society

The core of biblical history is the record of God's calling out a people for His name to represent His work on earth among men. The function of the church is not some isolated or detached program, but is an integral facet of God's plan to bring Redemption to man.

The New Testament church stands as a visible fulfillment of Christ's work; it is His *body*. Jesus said that His followers are in the world, but are not to be part of the world (John 17:15-18). Being in the world, the church functions as a new society. Unlike Israel that could function only in a singular culture and environment, the church is adaptable to any culture.

At the same time, the church is not of the world; therefore, it is not to be part of the world system. The church must protect itself not only from sin, but also from syncretism, the taking of non-Christian beliefs or practices and making them part of the church. The church can adapt to any cultural situation as long as it does not compromise the teachings of the Word of God.

The church functions as a dynamic enterprise

The church is primarily a dynamic representation of Christ and His work that can carry out realistically the Master's commission:

> *"All authority in heaven and on earth has been given to me. Therefore go and make disciples of all nations, baptizing them in the name of the Father and of the Son and of the Holy Spirit, and teaching them to obey everything I have commanded you. And surely I will be with*

you always, to the very end of the age" (Matt. 28:18-20).

Christ did not lay down an outline of doctrine and then invite those who believed it to form a fellowship on that basis. Rather, He communicated truth through personality in such a way that truth and fellowship were parts of one another and could not be separated. Jesus said, *"I am the way . . . I am the truth . . . I am the light"* (cf. John 8:12; 14:6). when He called His disciples it was to an experience of truth that became, by its own force, the ground of unity.

The early Christians had a dynamic experience of repentance and faith. It transformed them and brought new love that united them. Truth, to them, was not theoretical but real, dynamic, and experiential. John the Apostle wrote:

> *That which was from the beginning, which we have heard, which we have seen with our eyes, which we have looked at and our hands have touched—this we proclaim concerning the Word of life. We proclaim to you what we have seen and heard, so that you also may have fellowship with us. And our fellowship is with the Father and with his Son, Jesus Christ* (1 John 1:1, 3).

Bound to the Lord Jesus Christ by a common faith, the early Christians were bound also to one another. In this position they confronted the bitter hatred and opposition of the Jews, the forces of the Romans who sought to crush them, and the contempt of the Greeks who laughed them to scorn. They believed that truth in Jesus Christ would bring to light its own vindication and fight its own battles. Thus, the Apostle Paul said that *God was pleased through the foolishness of what was preached to save those who believe* (1 Cor. 1:21); he preached a simple gospel without respect to the age or its prejudices.

Without such conviction born of experience, the early church might have been united in name but not in reality. They truly were of *one body and one Spirit . . . one Lord, one faith, one baptism; one God and Father of all, who is over all and through all and in all* (Eph. 4:4-6).

Inherent in the church's own existence was a dynamic quality that had a divine freedom and flexibility. When Christ appointed twelve disciples, they bore a special significance and had special functions, but did not create a special order of successors or transmit their authority to anyone or to any particular office. Christ had instructed His disciples to wait for the Father's promised gift, the Holy Spirit, who would come *in a few days*, and then they would receive power and become His *witnesses in Jerusalem, in all Judea and Samaria, and to the ends of the earth* (Acts 1:5, 8).

It was the dynamic of the Holy Spirit and the special providence of God, not a fixed order of apostleship, that marked the early church. Paul maintained strenuously an apostleship that was neither from men nor through men (Gal. 1:1). He indicated that he consulted no man concerning his call to preach the gospel to the Gentiles (Gal. 1:16). It was the church of Antioch—not the Jerusalem church or even the apostles—that delegated Paul and Barnabas to their missionary task. When the church fasted and prayed, the Holy Spirit moved them to send Paul and Barnabas (Acts 13:1-2).

Paul touches upon the apparent personal influence and eminence of Peter, James, and John at Jerusalem—but does not mention their authority—at the time that he and Barnabas came to seek their right hand of fellowship. Paul had found it necessary to withstand Peter, the most outstanding leader and spokesman of the first church at Jerusalem. Although Peter had eaten with the Gentiles before in Antioch, when Judaizers came from Jerusalem and withdrew over a Jewish custom of certain foods, he also withdrew and ate separately. For this, Paul opposed Peter publicly and made it abundantly clear that it was an enterprise of the Holy Spirit, not humanly vested rights and interests, that directed the church (Gal. 2:6-16).

The New Testament ministry was not a priesthood specially constituted; grace was from above and not dispensed humanly. There simply were gifts that had been set in the church, having special functions that Christ had given sovereignly by the Holy Spirit, which, under His exercise, became authoritative.

No church had jurisdiction over other churches. What Paul taught in one church as a function of ministry he taught in all churches (1 Cor. 4:17; 16:1).

Problems within a local church at Antioch brought a request to the elders and apostles of Jerusalem. A council session was held, over which Pastor James of the Jerusalem church presided. The elders and apostles of Jerusalem and the delegates of Antioch were there, as was the whole church of Jerusalem, to consider the problem of circumcision, which had arisen because certain contentious Jews had come from Jerusalem to disturb the church at Antioch. The church at Jerusalem then assured the delegates of Antioch that these contentious men had not been sent by them and that the advice was not of authoritative or superior command but what seemed good for the unity of the church and to the Holy Spirit (Acts 15:1-29).

This unique dynamic of the Holy Spirit in the midst of the church, constituted as God's enterprise over which Christ was Lord, made the church function. The church is ordered and organized by the will and authority of the King whose love founded it, whose Spirit fills and guides it, and whose life quickens and enables its members.

The church functions as a unit

The organization of the church was not without tradition or design. There was unity and continuity felt by those who made up the church.

Unity and continuity characterized Christ's method. The primary image of the church centered in the ministry of Christ, whose message was proclaimed and whose body was represented. After His baptism *Jesus began to preach, "Repent, for the kingdom of heaven is near."* Immediately He called disciples whom He promised to make fishers of men, and then He went about in Galilee, teaching in the synagogues and preaching the gospel of the kingdom (Matt. 4:17-19, 23).

The English word *preach* may be used to translate two different Greek words in the original: *kerussein,* meaning "to herald," and *evangelizesthai,* meaning "to proclaim glad tidings" or "to evangelize." Jesus Christ was resolute in heralding the gospel. Simultaneously, He was notably aggressive in that He chose His disciples *that they might be with him and that he might send them out to preach* (Mark 3:14), thus to multiply His ministry.

In none of the Gospels, however, was Jesus called a

"preacher" *(kerux)*, nor was the delivery of His message called "preaching" *(kerugma)*. Forty-two times, however, He is called a "teacher." The message Jesus preached always was accompanied by teaching, and He continued to teach those who acknowledged Him as Messiah.

The nearer Christ came to the cross, the more His preaching and evangelizing became absorbed in teaching. He spent more time in teaching the Twelve to prepare them for ministry than in any other activity. He called His followers "disciples," meaning "learners," and in His last commission He commanded them to disciple all the nations by preaching, baptizing, and teaching.

To the Twelve Jesus taught a principle that became difficult for them to learn but which became central to the life of the church:

"You know that the rulers of the Gentiles lord it over them, and their high officials exercise authority over them. Not so with you. Instead, whoever wants to become great among you must be your servant, and whoever wants to be first must be your slave—just as the Son of Man did not come to be served, but to serve, and to give his life as a ransom for many" (Matt. 20:25-28).

Time and again desire for position and rank crept in upon the disciples (e.g., Matt. 18:1 ff.; 20:17 ff.). John wrote that this happened on the Passover night when Jesus girded Himself and washed the feet of the disciples (John 13:12-16).

Jesus taught a principle of service, designed to fortify and herald the gospel. This became the primary image of the early church.

Paul loved to call himself a slave *(doulos)*. Peter exhorted pastors not to be lords over God's heritage but good servants and exhorted Christians to be subject to one another and in brotherly love to serve one another (1 Pet. 5). So also Paul exhorted Christians to subjection and service.

The early church understood and practiced the principles Jesus had taught. In the Upper Room, Matthias was chosen as the servant fit to succeed Judas by a procedure that kept the principle intact. The first seven deacons were chosen by the whole multitude of believers at Jerusalem not for rank but for their natural and spiritual fitness (Acts 6:3-6).

It is interesting to note that on the day of Pentecost the principles Jesus used and taught are recognizable immediately within the body of believers (see Acts 2):

- preaching of the Word (v.37)
- repentance (v. 38)
- baptism (vv. 38, 41)
- continuance in the teaching and fellowship of the apostles (v. 42)
- breaking of bread and prayers (v. 42)
- the Lord adding to their number those who were being saved through their corporate witness (v. 47).

The thought of the church as a school runs through all of Paul's writing. Upon his conversion he began teaching in the synagogues and preaching (Acts 9:20 ff.). It appears he found it necessary to spend three years preparing himself in solitude (Gal. 1:17). Soon after, he is listed among the prophets and teachers at Antioch.

In his missionary ministry Paul sought to establish churches everywhere he went (Acts 16:5). He saw to it that in every place elders were appointed who were properly qualified and able to hold faithfully to the Word according to the teaching and able also to exhort in sound doctrine and to handle unruly men who were vain talkers and deceivers (Titus 1:9-10). Paul likewise exhorted Timothy to commit his teaching to other men who were able to teach others (2 Tim. 2:2).

Biblical descriptions of the functions of the church and the ministry relate more often to learning and to sharing what is learned than to any other factor. The church was a school of Christian living and witnessing. To be a believer and to live in a certain locality meant that one should unite with other believers in that place to form a base of operation. Thus, churches were established and became self-responsible units.

No doubt the organizational structure of the early church varied. No rigid polity ruled the people; the people came first. Their methods or polities were designed by principle to articulate and organize the energies manifested by the Spirit.

The Emphases of
the Church's Function

The various activities in the ministry of the early church no doubt would be quite extensive if they could be described in detail. Enough is given to recognize that the early converts had a strong consciousness of calling and relationship to Christ that governed all their activity. Several priorities of activity are obvious.

Evangelism

The task of proclamation and witness with a view to persuasion is primary in the church. The early church believed that the whole world was in a great emergency through sin and stood in need of the compassion God had shown in the death of His Son.

The New Testament gospel is the good news that the plan of Redemption has now been culminated in Christ. Christ had come to declare that the kingdom of God is at hand—at hand in His own person. His death and Resurrection made the seal of Redemption possible. Christ sent the Holy Spirit to give witness to this seal and to form a new community of fellowship called "the church" by which the gospel of the kingdom should be preached in all the world for a witness, and then the end would come (Matt. 24:14).

Evangelism is divine compassion made relevant to a lost world through redeemed people empowered by the Holy Spirit, teaching the Word of God. Jesus outlined the program of reaching the unreached as preaching, baptizing, teaching, and causing the reached to observe what He commanded.

The church's principal task, in fact its business, is to save the lost, even as Jesus had come into the world to save sinners.

Worship and nurture

While evangelism is the primary work of the church, worship and nurture cannot be neglected in its pursuit. There is always the need of growing in grace and in the knowledge of Christ, owning the lordship of Christ, and coming to know the full provision of the Holy Spirit for life and power.

Evangelism will deteriorate unless the converts are baptized and taught the full responsibility of obeying Christ in all things and then are shown how to obey. The converts of the early church learned the apostles' doctrine and fellowship and became steadfast in their worship (Acts 2:42, 46-47).

The earliest Christians met together for what is described as "meeting for the Word," the purpose of which was for edification (Gal. 6:6; Phil. 2:16; Col. 1:6; 3:16; 1 Thess. 1:5-6; 2:13; 1 Tim. 5:17; Titus 1:9). Some aspects of their services are discernible, although their order is not:

- prayer (1 Cor. 11:4; 14:12 ff.; 2 Cor. 9:12-14)
- singing *psalms, hymns and spiritual songs* (1 Cor. 14:26; Eph. 5:19; Col. 3:16)
- reading of apostolic letters, perhaps regularly (Col. 4:16; 1 Thess. 5:27)
- teaching, possibly a reiteration of tradition concerning faith and conduct (1 Tim. 4:6-11; Titus 2:11-15)
- prophecy, or the preaching of the Word as revelation according to the proportion of faith, as Paul puts it (Acts 13:1; 15:32; 22:3 ff.; 26:12 ff.; Rom. 12:6; 1 Cor. 12:1 ff.; 13:2; Gal. 1:12)
- tongues; this caused confusion at Corinth—Paul did not forbid it in church services but gave it faint praise (1 Cor. 14:12-19)
- collection upon the first day of the week (1 Cor. 16:1-2)
- the Lord's Supper—it appears that this observance was practiced in several kinds of meetings. The tradition that Paul received was simple (1 Cor. 11:23-27), but a common meal was sometimes followed by the Lord's Supper as at Corinth (1 Cor. 11:18, 20, 34). Regular participation in the services of the church was part of the Christian Way. Through this they worshiped and were built up in their faith.

Service

When the early Christians obeyed the leading of the Spirit of Christ, they went everywhere to witness and do good even as their Master had done (Acts 10:38). They shared generously (Acts 2:45; Eph. 4:28); cared for the widows (Acts 6:1; 1

Tim. 5:3); labored in prayer (Acts 4:24-31; 12:5); generally were exhorted to do good, particularly to the household of faith (Gal. 6:10; Eph. 6:7); were known for their goodness (Acts 9:36; 11:24; Rom. 14:16; Eph. 2:10); and ministered the Word by life and testimony so that they went everywhere witnessing (Acts 5:42; 15:21).

Interspersed in the book of Acts are the following statements indicative of the earnestness of activity among the believers in their faithfulness to the Word and its witness: *The Word of God spread. The number of disciples . . . increased* (6:7). *But the word of God continued to increase and spread* (12:24). *The word of the Lord spread widely and grew in power* (19:20).

The Master had said, *"Whoever loses his life for my sake will find it"* (Matt. 10:39). Members of the New Testament church recognized their gifts and callings and invested all their interests in the work and labor of the church. The Apostle Paul exhorted the Corinthians always to give themselves fully to the work of the Lord because they could be sure that their labor in the Lord was not in vain (1 Cor. 15:58).

Growth in grace also involves service, and without service faith is dead—being alone, *as the body without the spirit is dead* (James 2:26).

The Objectives of the Church's Function

The immediate and long-range objectives of the church can be discerned in the Great Commission and in Acts 1:8: *"But you will receive power when the Holy Spirit comes on you; and you will be my witnesses in Jerusalem, and in all Judea and Samaria, and to the ends of the earth."* Two aspects are recognized in this all-inclusive objective.

Reach the community

The church is a fellowship of believers who bear witness in the locality in which they live. The New Testament church loses its significance when it fails to bear fruit by means of an effective witness in its own locality. The church is to represent in the community *the pillar and foundation of the truth* (1 Tim. 3:15). Oneness between believers in Christ is to function in such a way that unbelievers will be persuaded. As the result of the early church's demonstration of Christian unity and life, souls were added to their number daily, and we begin to read of "churches" plural instead of "church" singular.

Roland Leavell has written:

Scriptural evangelism is planned, promoted and conserved by the churches. Individual Christians are the evangelists; yet all the results of their evangelism should go into the church life for its strength and power. The Church is the promotional organization for the advancement of the kingdom of God, even as the individual Christian is the promotional unit. Any evangelism which does not strengthen the Church, bring people into the Church, and advance the kingdom of God through the Church is seriously lacking some of the essentials of scriptural evangelism *(Evangelism, Christ's Imperative Commission:* Nashville, Tenn.: Broadman Press, 1951, p. 20).

The church has a responsibility to the local community, and believers have responsibility to the church in reaching the local community.

Reach the ends of the earth

The church has a twofold responsibility—at home and overseas. Jesus said, *"You will be my witnesses in Jerusalem, and in all Judea and Samaria, and to the ends of the earth"* (Acts 1:8). The impact of the double responsibility must be understood, particularly where the gospel has not been preached and churches have not been firmly grounded. Jesus did not anticipate total evangelization in Jerusalem before Samaria should hear.

Mark says of the first believers: *Then the disciples went out and preached everywhere* (16:20). Luke reveals that *those who had been scattered preached the word wherever they went* (Acts 8:4). The record of the book of Acts serves as a sample. Jerusalem was the starting point. From there Philip went to Samaria. Peter was called to go to Caesarea.

63

Peter, like most of the first Christians, was a Jew. His tradition and background accepted the view that all followers of Jehovah must become Jews, but when the Holy Spirit dealt with him through the conversion of Cornelius (Acts 10), new light from old truth Jesus had taught dawned on him: God is no respecter of persons, *but accepts men from every nation who fear him and do what is right* (Acts 10:35).

The rigid tradition of the Jerusalem church, however, hindered its broad missionary responsibility.

Though Barnabas had been sent from Jerusalem to Antioch, where many Greeks had been converted, to supervise that congregation (Acts 11:22), Antioch soon succeeded Jerusalem. From there Paul made three extensive missionary tours through Asia Minor and into Europe.

Paul's passion for the missionary enterprise carried him to the whole known world, involving shipwrecks, imprisonments, riots, hunger, and physical weakness. The wider his experience the greater became his ministry and blessing. To the Romans he wrote:

> *For there is no difference between Jew and Gentile— the same Lord is Lord of all and richly blesses all who call on him, for, "Everyone who calls on the name of the Lord will be saved."*
>
> *How, then, can they call on the one they have not believed in? And how can they believe in the one of whom they have not heard? And how can they hear without someone preaching to them? And how can they preach unless they are sent?* (Rom. 10:12-15).

The desire to reach others outside their immediate community was true of the groups at Ephesus, Philippi, and Rome. Everywhere Christianity proved capable of transforming the hearts and minds of men and of renovating society. Most of the congregations established by missionary activity increased rapidly and spread to the surrounding communities. The writings of John to the seven churches surrounding Ephesus intimate and reflect activites concerning which little is recorded in other Scripture.

The Bible does not attempt to give a complete history of the church even in its own times, but it gives enough to reveal the program of missions God intended for the church to have and which His Spirit would bless. Total evangelization, not total Christianization, was the point of the Great Commission.

The church represents God's strategy for world evangelization. God's purpose in visiting the Gentiles was to take from them *a people for himself* (Acts 15:14).

In the parable of the sower Jesus illustrated that only a fourth of those who heard proved genuine (Matt. 13:3-8). In the parable of the tares He illustrated that Christianity would always be surrounded with evil (Matt. 13:24-30).

No community has been totally and permanently Christianized. The church always stands to face the enemy. Its design is to face the enemy and live dynamically as it fulfills a worldwide missionary function.

UNDERSTANDING THE CHURCH'S HISTORICAL DEVELOPMENT

Since it is the purpose of this book to understand The Christian and Missionary Alliance as a denomination today, we must understand both the scriptural and the historical church patterns. Any interpretation of church history since the close of the New Testament canon does not have the same authority as the revelation itself, but new graphic lessons are made apparent as the hand of God in the ultimate accomplishment of His redemptive plan and purpose is traced.

God's standard of truth applied to church history becomes a significant factor in understanding my church. All of individual life and the corporate life of the church would lose their meaning if this were not possible.

All history and inspired revelation are correlated in God's perspective. The church as people and as an institution of society is as important now as the day it was born. To refuse to accept the church's identity or one's responsibility to it is tantamount to denying the function and purpose of Scripture and the living reality of Jesus Christ himself.

The immediate purpose of this section is to form a bridge between the church of New Testament times and The Christian and Missionary Alliance and to be as open to New Testament revelation as God enables us to see it. Though our understanding of it will necessarily be imperfect, every effort should be made to trace the finger of God and to appreciate every insight the Holy Spirit gives.

5

The Post-New
Testament Era
of the Church

Under pressure of time the church undergoes constant changes. This was true throughout New Testament times and has been ever since.

The church as an institution has accumulated many false accretions like barnacles that cling to a ship. There have been times in church history when the unfriendly world expected the church to flounder and disappear from sight. Nevertheless, Jesus promised that the gates of hell would not prevail against His church (Matt. 16:18) and this gospel of the kingdom would be preached in the whole world as a testimony to all nations, and then the end would come (Matt. 24:14).

Jesus Christ looked upon the church with a positive vision and likened it to the relationship of husband and wife in marriage:

Christ loved the church and gave himself up for her to make her holy, cleansing her by the washing with water through the word, and to present her to himself as a radiant church, without stain or wrinkle or any other blemish, but holy and blameless (Eph. 5:25-27).

In the last chapter and the last verses of the New Testament is this invitation:

The Spirit and the bride ₍the church₎ say, "Come!" And let him who hears say, "Come!" Whoever is thirsty, let him come; and whoever wishes, let him take the free gift of the water of life (Rev. 22:17).

However dark some periods of church history may appear, the ultimate promise and vision of Christ will be fully vindicated.

The End of the Apostolic Period

The last surviving apostle was John, who wrote one of the Gospels, three epistles, and The Revelation. According to tradition, he died about A.D. 98 at the age of one hundred. A number of post-New Testament writers wrote extrabiblical accounts that speak of him as having been bishop at Ephesus. The book of Revelation, according to tradition, was written in the later years of Domitian, about A.D. 95, from the Isle of Patmos where John was exiled for his faith.

The transition

As we piece biblical history together with secular sources, we discover a number of happenings. When Paul was arrested in Jerusalem, he was taken finally to Rome (A.D. 62-63) and held prisoner (Acts 21, 28) until in A.D. 68, when he died a martyr's death at the hand of Nero.

Nero's top general, Vespasian (A.D. 69-79), became the emperor and, in A.D. 70, he sent an officer named Titus with 60,000 troops to put down an insurrection of the Jews. Tens of thousands of Jews were slain, 100,000 were taken captive, and Jerusalem was thoroughly demolished, as Christ had predicted (Matt. 24:1-3).

Vespasian's reign was followed by the reigns of Titus (A.D. 79-81) and Domitian (A.D. 81-96). Domitian's tyrannical reign, plagued with incessant crimes and cruelties, is believed to have been one of the worst. The persecution went on for 250 years. It is estimated that 750,000 Christians were martyred. Christians were torn to pieces by dogs, burned at the stake, and tortured beyond belief, but the church persevered.

A new suffering servant

Not much is known beyond the biblical account of the

labors of the other apostles who died before John, the apostle. Hegesippus and Eusebius in their writings give what tradition they knew.

It is believed that Thomas labored in India, Philip in Phrygia, Simon Zelotes in Egypt, Andrew in Asia Minor and Greece, Matthias in Ethiopia, Judas Thaddeus in Persia, and Bartholomew in Armenia and India. This tradition reflects the apostles' obedience to the Great Commission. The spread of Christianity that followed testifies to the effectiveness of their ministry along with the ministry of the churches they established. God's strategy for world evangelization was confirmed. The church was the new suffering servant reflecting her Lord.

The book of Acts has a stronger message than merely facts of history often treated superficially. In Acts, the main enemies of the church were the people entrenched in Judaistic tradition. The persecution by non-Christian Gentiles was spasmodic and usually designed to please the Jews. Jesus predicted that the time would come when those who would kill His disciples would think they were doing God a service (John 16:2).

The record remains, however, that the early church, as God's servant-people, had power. The Thessalonian populace voiced a popular complaint: *These men who have caused trouble all over the world have now come here* (Acts 17:6). These people were in touch with God.

The Period of the Church Fathers

From the period of the apostles to the time of Augustine (A.D. 354-430), fierce conflict forced the church to wage war on two fronts, persecution from without and heresy from within. Most of what we know came from men of stature who stood out as protectors of the church. They have been called "church fathers," not just because of their proximity to the New Testament period but because of their courageous and knowledgeable defense of Christianity. With remarkable spiritual character they were to guide the future of the church.

The Roman world

When Christianity began its conquest, Roman rule was universal. The Greeks gave literature and religion a philosophical bent, but the Romans gave everything a practical turn, particularly government. Learned Jews of Alexandria, such as Philo, developed a philosophy that tried to combine the religion and philosophy of the Greeks with Judaism and Christianity. They endeavored to bring the best of Egyptian, Roman, and Oriental strains into harmony.

The various types of religious heresy that tried to use Christianity and to pervert it constitutes an involved study. Suffice it to say that many early church fathers, especially Irenaeus (d. A.D. 202), made great efforts to suppress and uproot heresy

Justin Martyr (circa A.D. 100-165) tried out the various systems of heathen philosophy in vain until he finally found peace in Christianity and became a great defender of the Christian faith.

Tertullian (circa A.D. 150-220) received a good classical education and became a lawyer. Converted at the age of forty, he became a Christian orator and writer of first rank.

Clement of Rome, Polycarp of Smyrna, Clement and Origen of Alexandria, and others, all lived early in the second century and wrote great works in defense of Christianity.

The early Christians did not relish the suspicion, ridicule, contempt, and ostracism they suffered. The powerful sanctions of public opinion represented a stronger inhibition than the lions, flames, and crucifixions Rome used to enforce the state religion that was to cement the unity of the empire.

Because they met in secret, the Christians often were accused of immorality. The gospel of the cross and the practice of the Lord's table produced such false reports as human sacrifice and the drinking of blood. Christians were rumored to plot against Caesar in order to establish a new kingdom. The heathen populace blamed earthquakes, famines, floods, and storms on Christians. When the empire was threatened by barbarian tribes to the north it was convenient to attack Christianity as a scapegoat in order to marshal the various countries in support of the throne. In this environment and climate the church fathers became renowned.

The sudden rise and power of the church

Under the pressure of persecution Christians manifested the grace of God. Their courage in the face of death gave credence to their beliefs. Their allegiance to the Lord Jesus Christ and His teachings had a strong positive effect on the society of the first century.

Slavery was universal in A.D. 300. Attica is said to have had twenty thousand slaves. Pagans commonly held wives as slaves. What contrast to the Christian teaching that in Christ is neither bond nor free, male nor female! (Gal. 3:28) How beautiful Paul's statement to Philemon concerning the runaway slave Onesimus: *So if you consider me a partner, welcome him as you would welcome me!* (Philem. 17)

In the second century even more people in the upper classes accepted the gospel.

As the number of Christians increased, persecution became more severe until whole towns were wiped out. Finally, Diocletian (A.D. 284-305), instigator of this holocaust, gave up trying to drown Christianity in blood and was forced to abdicate the throne.

Shortly afterward, Constantine came to the throne and in A.D. 313 issued the Edict of Milan, proclaiming liberty of conscience and making Christianity a legalized religion. He promoted Christian teaching, exempted Christian clergy from military duty and taxation, enjoined the observance of Sunday, and contributed to the building of Christian places of worship. Seeing Christianity as a powerful support of the state, he gave it popularity and power. Forty-two years later Theodosius I suppressed pagan religions and made Christianity the only official religion.

The sudden fall and weakness of the church

When Jesus said, *"Woe to you when all men speak well of you"* (Luke 6:26), it was no idle warning. The triumph of the church became absorbed in the triumph of the state; great evils followed. Union of church and state made centralization of church power a matter of course.

With the establishment of a celibate priesthood, the priests distorted the pastor-elder office and drew apart from lay elders and deacons. They reserved for themselves the rights of ordination and control of finances. Gradually they developed a hierarchy. The concept of salvation changed so that the priesthood mediated salvation. Baptism and the Lord's Supper became saving sacraments instead of symbolic ordinances.

Perhaps the most devastating development was a ceremonialism that eclipsed education. The teaching function of the church almost disappeared because the priesthood regulated the spiritual and moral life of the people with the sacraments and the Bible was withdrawn from the people on the ground that only the priests were qualified interpreters.

The Medieval Era

The Roman Empire, full of internal corruption and harassed by Germanic peoples, began to collapse after A.D. 410. In many ways it had been ideal for the diffusion of the gospel. Roman law assimilated conquered peoples and created a well-regulated citizenry. The government maintained good roads and maritime commerce and developed facility in communication, since Greek in the East and Latin in the West were official languages that interlaced the empire.

Even the imperial suppression of Christianity had been a blessing in disguise. Intolerance made for solidarity; evangelistic and missionary activities were guarded from superficialities by the threat of martyrdom.

The sudden change and the development of the Roman Catholic church created new problems for which the remnant of true believers was unprepared. By the fifth century, the church was rent with controversies and heresies. Vigorous protests by dissenting elements were held in check by manipulating leverages of power.

The new ecclesiastical power structures sought governmental association and protection wherever it could be found. The Eastern church under the Byzantine Empire became disassociated from the Roman church, while in many areas where the Goths, the Vandals, and the Huns had taken control the church sought to Christianize and provide what order it could.

The Eastern church

As Western civilization under the influence of Christianity began to move toward its own center and the main polarization of the church was between the East and the West, the inherent differences in the Oriental language, lifestyle, and environment became more pronounced in the Eastern church. In A.D. 692, it established canons in its own synods that sanctioned marriage for the lower clergy, which had been prohibited under the Roman Catholic church. The patriarch of Constantinople was given equal rank with the pope at Rome and forbade the pictorial and image representation of Christ.

The Eastern church became strong in Oriental mysticism and ceremonialism and began to withdraw from the progressive elements that had characterized the Roman world. For many, the deserts of Asia and Egypt became a refuge from the fate of society. Monasticism began to flourish.

The Eastern more than the Western church was satisfied with promoting the cult of its practice rather than seeking theological understanding. Instead of being a servant-people to meet the needs of a lost world with God's plan of Redemption, the Eastern church became a self-serving people made up of strange religious elements, and thus lost the dynamic of the gospel.

The Western church

As the Germanic tribes moved southward, the bishops of Rome began to exercise civil as well as ecclesiastical authority. Many of the Goths and Huns who captured Rome and broke up the western empire were baptized. Inadequate teaching and lawlessness gave rise to superstition and guerilla warfare so that feudal lordships with large estates were formed. This served as a form of protection for the common people who became vassals while monarchs and pontiffs vied for authority.

For a thousand years after Rome fell, Europe became a vast region of darkness. Sometimes in the monastery where St. Jerome was translating the Bible or Bernard of Clairvaux was composing verse for hymnody or in a place of social prominence where St. Francis of Assisi was renouncing affluence to bring life and discipline to the church or in a cathedral where Anselm was writing a discourse about divine grace, the shafts of light broke through the dark clouds.

The church, perverted in the understanding of its function, tried to regain the Holy Land from the Muslims by sponsoring crusades. Feudal nobility raised armies and captured Jerusalem in 1099 in a terrible slaughter, but by 1291 the western holdings were lost under the persistent pressure of the Muslims. An estimated million Christians and Muslims lost their lives. During this period special orders of a monastic nature developed while the church extended its catholicism with ecclesiastical machinery.

Roman Catholicism

When Christ left His disciples, He left only a basic outline for the organization of the church. As the church gained favor, it tended to adapt the structures of the governmental systems then used. The bishop of Rome, the pope, corresponded to the position of the emperor; cardinals, to that of the Roman curia. Metropolitan bishops and archbishops imitated the provincial governments and priests became local officers by whom the masses were held in a religious slavery that was worse than the Roman slavery during the early church period.

The church's dominance led to full acceptance by the government; in fact, as noted earlier, it became the only legal religion. In this exalted status it had numerous privileges including immunity from taxes on ever-growing estates. Eventually the church was allowed to impose its own taxes and to govern with the same authority and power as civil law.

This kind of power helped corrupt the church and led to a number of abuses, the chief of which was simony, or the buying and selling of church offices. Even the sacramental system of seven sacraments—ordination, baptism, confirmation, penance, extreme unction, marriage, and the Holy Eucharist—was used for revenue purposes. Excessive fees were charged for burials. Penance could be obtained by monetary payment. Special indulgences or letters of pardon were sold for the purpose of using the money gained to build cathedrals and to support the scandalous luxury of the papal court.

In a military spirit like that developed during the Crusades, critics of the church were easily branded as heretics and public enemies. Sometimes these were silenced by excommunication. Where this was not sufficient, the state stepped in to seize the critic as a public enemy and to execute him.

In 1208, Pope Innocent III formally set up the Inquisition, a special tribunal that ruthlessly plunged large areas of southern France, northern Spain, and northern Italy into a blood bath. Heretics in these areas were pursued with relentless cruelty for a century. Those who directed the Inquisition were given special indulgences.

Corruption and cruelty earmarked the Roman church until the sixteenth century. From 1305 to 1377 the papacy was subject to the French court and the papal palace was in Avignon. From 1377 to 1417 there were two popes, at Avignon and at Rome, each claiming to be the "vicar of Christ" and with each excommunicating the other. Finally, a third compromise pope was elected and eventually the whole matter was settled with the Roman pope gaining full power.

The kinds of wranglings and abuses as noted above plagued the church and helped to set the stage for the impact of the Reformation.

6

The Reformational Setting of the Church

The Reformation did not come as a sudden bolt out of the blue. Conditions had been ripening in which the needs for reform and open protest in defiance of the whole papal system became inevitable. Truth may go underground, but it finally will prevail. No doubt the papal schism between Avignon and Rome opened the way for the expression of dissenters.

Forerunners of the Reformation

There were those within the Catholic church who had begun to reach for spiritual reality. Among them were the German mystics who discovered a biblical pattern that disclosed the reality of God.

Dissenters

Johannes Eckhart, a Dominican monk, preached in the German vernacular on the reality of God. Johannes Tauler, a disciple of Eckhart, preached biblical salvation messages for the conversion of sinners. Thomas A'Kempis, a copyist of Scripture from the order of the Brethren of the Common Life, discovered the reality of Jesus Christ and wrote the classic *The Imitation of Christ*. There was wheat among the chaff in the medieval church.

Dissenting groups, like the Albigenses and Waldenses, were led by intelligent researchers of truth. John Wycliff (1324-1384), a teacher at Oxford, England, began a movement that taught that the individual needed no clerical mediator between himself and God. Advocating the right of the people to read the Bible for themselves, he translated it into the English language.

John Huss (1369-1415), rector of the University of Prague in Bohemia, became a fearless preacher, condemning the sale of indulgences and exalting the Scriptures above dogmas and canons of the church. He paid for his daring by being burned at the stake.

Girolamo Savonarola (1452-1498) was probably the most powerful preacher before the times of Martin Luther and John Calvin. To thousands who thronged his cathedral he preached against sin and papal vice until revival came to the city of Florence. The pope tried to silence him with a bribe, but, finally, the reformer was hanged and then burned in the square in Florence.

The Anabaptists, another dissident movement, were devoted to the Scriptures. They possessed certain affinities with medieval renewal groups and became influential early in the sixteenth century. The Anabaptists infiltrated various European countries including Switzerland, Austria, Germany, and, in particular, Holland. They stressed separation of church and state and rejected infant baptism, from which they got the name *Anabaptists* (those who baptize again).

These are but a sample of the many dissenting elements that were becoming the rising tide.

The Renaissance

A revival of learning was occasioned, in part, by the Crusades. Cross-cultural encounter aroused a spirit of inquiry, a search for freedom, and a realization that in the antiquity of Greece and the Far East a thousand years previously, learning had surpassed that which the present culture knew. Industry, science, commerce, and exploration opened many new areas of understanding and brought about a new balance of power that helped to pave the way for the Reformation.

There arose a passion for the ancient classics. Libraries were founded and many ancient manuscripts were collected. The printing press was invented and the first publication, in 1453, was the Gutenberg Bible. From 1450 to 1520 the popes entered into the spirit of the Renaissance and surrounded themselves with artists, scholars, and linguists who revived interest in the study of Hebrew and Greek. This promoted a fuller understanding of the Bible on which the reforms of Luther, Zwingli, and Calvin were based.

The Reformation

While many forces had been at work to prepare the way, it took a bold and noble champion to set the image and cause of the Reformation. It was the blast of Luther's trumpet that marshaled those forces to full attention and startled many countries out of their sleep.

Martin Luther (1483-1546)

The beginning of the Reformation is dated usually from October 31, 1517, the day that Martin Luther publicly nailed a copy of his ninety-five Theses on the massive door of the Wittenberg Church. This act was a protest mainly against indulgences. Luther was ready to defend his stand against any and all opponents. His thoughts were born of a long inner conflict over the question of salvation. No doubt Luther was surprised over the tumult his action raised, but he was of a character and temperament that would not retreat easily when the issues of battle were joined.

Although Luther considered himself a good Catholic and not consciously hostile to either church or pope, his conviction had graduated to an irrevocable stand. God, in His providence, had found a champion for the truth that would extol salvation through grace alone, based on the Word of God.

Luther's political aid and protection from Prince Frederick, a territorial monarch under the German king, Charles V, provided an advantage that enabled him to propagate and defend his stand on biblical truth. So overwhelming were the odds against Luther that only miraculous circumstances saved the Protestant cause.

Luther enlarged his evangelical convictions. Basing his stand on the Scriptures, he rejected special priesthood, the whole sacramental system, and purgatory. One of Luther's great contributions was the translation of the Bible into German. The Reformation entered Spain, Italy, and France and received political support in the Scandinavian countries and Switzerland.

In Switzerland the cantons, or territorial districts, formed a federation of defense that was championed by a reformer named Ulrich Zwingli, a young man fired by the spirit of renaissance and a firm believer in a democratic system of government. He ridiculed the ecclesiastical abuses of the Catholic church and accepted the doctrinal views of Luther with the exception of the nature of the Lord's table.

For a time the Protestant cause lost momentum as Catholic and Protestant factions fought each other. But during the middle of the sixteenth century, new strength and enlargement came from the direction of Geneva.

John Calvin (1509-1564)

John Calvin, an adept intellectual with an introspective, syllogistic mind trained in universities of Paris and Orleans, was forced to flee from France for his heretical views. He went to Geneva in 1534. With unusual ability and strength he became the commanding figure in that free city republic. With a strong sense of mission he undertook to make Geneva like the original church of Christ with a relentless care for the morals and beliefs of its citizens.

Calvin's central concern was to reconstruct an evangelical edifice, and his main contribution was to reduce the Protestant revolt to a theological coherence. This he did in his *Institutes of the Christian Religion.* By this work he sought to persuade the world that the Protestant faith should not be persecuted. The first six chapters were published when Calvin had reached the age of twenty-six. From then until his death, at age fifty-five, he kept adding and expanding until 104 chapters were completed and put into four volumes. To this day the *Institutes* remain the classic of Protestant works on Christian doctrine.

Calvin made contributions in three particular areas: church government, morals, and theology. He believed that democracy was the system of government practiced in the primitive church and thereby made a popular appeal that was absent in Lutheranism.

Concerning morals, he believed that life should be lived for the glory of God and in the consciousness of God's active and sufficient grace. It was not a hierarchy but individuals who made up the church, and the strength of the individuals made for the strength of the church.

In theology, Lutheranism often had the tendency to extol faith as an end in itself whereas Calvinism directed the focus to God as all-sufficient, acting in pure mercy through Jesus Christ to exemplify godliness in daily living.

John Knox (1515-1572)

John Knox, priest in Scotland, began preaching reformation ideas about 1540. He visited Geneva and absorbed Calvinist teaching. Through his influence reform movements in both government and church became closely associated, and a Presbyterian form of church government was organized throughout Scotland. His intuitive leadership ability gave spiritual direction to the entire nation.

Though the Reformation in no way can be confined to the leadership of Luther, Calvin, and Knox, they form, perhaps, the most influential background to the future of the evangelical church.

The Post-Reformation Period

The influence of the Reformation on nation after nation in Europe changed the complexion of Western civilization. The strong countermeasures developed by the Roman Catholic church managed to stop the Reformation in southern Europe. In the North, the Reformation shaped the state churches and had a definite influence on these nations.

The Counter-Reformation

The Reformation made inroads into the unity of the Roman Catholic church, bringing about what is known as the Counter-Reformation. The Catholic church began to recognize abuses that needed correction as well as the theological weaknesses that fed the opposition.

For eighteen years the Council of Trent met intermittently to try to bring about a new united front to the Roman church. This Council did correct some abuses such as the outlawing of simony, but it also reiterated traditional doctrines such as tradition being equal to Scripture, indulgences, and the sacramental system as being essential to salvation. A confession of faith summarizing the doctrines of the church was completed.

The strongest impetus to the Roman Catholic Counter-Reformation was the Jesuits under the leadership of Ignatius Loyola. This organization had a regimented structure with discipline as strict as any army. This group stopped the spread of Protestantism in southern Europe. It also established excellent schools and pioneered Catholic missions in India, Japan, China, and the New World. Jesuits often were appointed as the private chaplains of the Catholic monarchs of Europe.

The efforts of the Counter-Reformation carved out southern Europe—roughly along the lines of the Holy Roman Empire—as a Roman Catholic enclave that has remained such to this day. Church and state became more tightly interwoven. As a result, a permanent bond was established in these areas.

The Reformation spreads

The fifteenth and sixteenth centuries in Europe were marked by the rise of strong national states. As these states grew in power the church had to reckon with the situation. In all of Europe, state churches grew and paralleled the national state's growth. The primary issue after the Reformation was whether the state church would be Catholic or Protestant.

After years of open armed conflict, the issue of the legality of Lutheranism in Germany was settled by the Peace of Augsburg in 1555. By that action the prince of a province would decide the legal religion for his area. Generally,

Lutheranism became the prominent religion of the North; Catholicism, the South. Lutheranism spread to all of Scandinavia and through various acts, some with force, became the state church of those countries.

Again, after bloodshed, the Netherlands and Switzerland became Protestant and Belgium and France became Cathic. In France it was not until 1598 that the Huguenots, French Calvinists, gained legal status.

In England, King Henry VIII denounced the authority of the pope and made himself "head of the church." The conflict was over Henry's desire to have his marriage to Catherine of Aragon annulled so that he could remarry. She had failed to give him a male heir. The pope was then forced to choose between Henry VIII and Philip of Aragon (Spain). He aligned himself with the latter. Henry broke with Rome and established the Church of England.

The Church of England was established as the state church. Challenges from Catholics and Calvinists in the form of Puritans continued into the midseventeenth century. Not until after the ascension of William and Mary to the throne in 1688 was the issue finally settled that England would remain Protestant. It was not until the eighteenth century that religious freedom was granted to Catholics in England.

After struggling with the issue of Calvinism in the 1560s, Scotland, under the leadership of John Knox, also became Protestant, with the Church of Scotland (Presbyterian) established firmly.

The church in the New World

Discovery and exploration of the New World brought France, England, and Spain into a race for political and economic power. The American colonies accepted the European pattern of church and state combination, and nine of the thirteen colonies had state churches. Only Rhode Island practiced religious freedom; the other twelve had some restrictions on religious groups.

The immigrants to the New World were primarily religious dissenters. Puritans were Calvinists out of step with the Church of England. Quakers and Catholics had difficulty also because of the state church. Baptists, Pietists, Moravians, and other minority groups made their way west.

Not until the late eighteenth century did the ideas of religious freedom and separation of church and state take root. In the beginning groups like the Puritans fled persecution only to establish repressive state churches in the New World.

Virginia's "Declaration of Rights" in 1785 and the Bill of Rights in the Constitution a few years later established religious freedom and separation of church and state for the United States.

Canada and Latin America were established by Catholic countries, with Latin America remaining as such. After France ceded Canada to Great Britain in 1763, Protestantism prevailed in most areas of Canada.

7

The North American Setting of the Church

The immediate background forces that gave shape and form to The Christian and Missionary Alliance were not in view until the middle of the nineteenth century. Since New Testament times, however, the providence of God was at work to shape His church. There are families and tribes in God's church much as in Old Testament Israel, and each has but one standard—to be conformed to the image of Christ. No particular church can presume upon God's favor.

The church on the North American scene has many significant aspects. Before focusing on The Christian and Missionary Alliance, it is first necessary to consider those aspects of influence that seem most pertinent to our understanding of its immediate background.

Revivalism and the Influence of Pietism

As the church fails to resist the currents in which the perishing world is drifting, its very life root may be endangered. On the North American scene by the beginning of the eighteenth century, religious declension had set in seriously.

Revivalism
With declension came revival—local at first and then

spreading until it became known as "The Great Awakening." The Mennonites and Moravians in Pennsylvania and, particularly in the Dutch Reformed church, under the preaching of a German Pietist named Frelinghuysen experienced the first local revival. In 1728, the English and Scotch Presbyterians under Gilbert and William Tennent saw another outbreak of revival. The flame began to burn in New England in 1734, under the preaching of Jonathan Edwards.

In 1740, George Whitfield made his first of five preaching tours. He began at Philadelphia and proceeded north to Massachusetts. The local revivals merged and spread.

The Great Awakening was over by 1750. In the late eighteenth century Methodism grew rapidly. Its influence developed into the Second Great Awakening in the early 1800s. The revived church grew and spread westward. Modern overseas and home missions of the North American churches grew out of this revival movement.

Pietism's lengthy shadow

Recent research has observed Pietism's tremendous influence on the North American church. Beginning as a quiet movement among Lutherans in Germany, the Pietists reacted to formalism and intellectualism by stressing Bible study and personal experience with Christ.

Under the leadership of August Francke (1663-1735) and Jacob Spener (1635-1705), Pietism was partially the result of the influence of Calvinism and of German mystics such as Johannes Tauler. Spener spoke of the double office of faith, of justification that makes sinners righteous positionally and of sanctification that followed with the inward working of the Holy Spirit.

The Pietist lineage extended to the English Puritans, as reflected in Richard Baxter's *Saint's Rest*, Walter Marshall's *Gospel Mystery of Sanctification,* and Phillip Doddridge's *Rise and Progress of Religion in the Soul.* These books became prime reading in the Canadian household in which Albert B. Simpson, founder of The Christian and Missionary Alliance, was reared.

The Pietist influence extended also to the Moravians, the

Church of the Brethren, the Swedish Mission Friends, and the Wesleyan movement.

The Moravians, remnants of the Hussite Brethren, sought refuge in 1722 on the estate of Count Nicholas Zinzendorf. In 1727, the Moravian church was actually born. Moravians preached conversion and sanctification as necessary components of salvation and felt compelled to form groups within established churches to promote a deeper spiritual life and vision for missions. Their disregard for doctrinal formulas, formal training of ministers, and ecclesiastical structure hampered their long-range effectiveness, but their love for simple Bible study, witnessing, and missionary zeal gave them wide influence.

It was through the Moravians at Aldersgate in London that John Wesley, founder of Methodism, received assurance of salvation. He had been strongly influenced by the German mystics also through William Law, an Anglican who wrote *A Serious Call to a Devout and Holy Life.* He took issue with the Moravians regarding a critical sanctifying experience by giving Christ full preeminence. Wesley felt that further perfection of the soul was needed whereby the root of sin was either suspended or extinguished at a particular moment of spiritual experience. He never claimed to have achieved this experience but believed in its possibility.

The holiness message, however, found no clear expression until years later when a large and prosperous Methodism became divided by the inroads of modernism and liberalism.

Modernism and the Holiness Quest

During the industrial revolution, the larger Protestant denominations became more controlled by business methods. Great churches often were dominated by men of wealth. The services became more formal, while the laboring immigrant masses often were ignored. America was seeking to emulate England in its Victorian splendor while secularization and materialism were weakening the churches' vitals.

Modernism and liberalism
During the latter half of the nineteenth century, an in-

fluence more devastating than materialism and secularism crept into the church. At first almost unawares but then more and more brazenly, a movement called "liberalism" made its way into universities and seminaries. Initially it came mostly from Germany, then took hold in England, and, finally, came to America.

Proponents of liberalism, enamored by the possibilities of organic evolution, the power of experimental science, and the adequacy of human ethics, attacked the Bible as containing much that was untrue. The Genesis story, the virgin birth, the deity and Resurrection of Christ, and many other parts of Scripture contained supernatural elements that did not harmonize with new learning. Liberalism claimed the right of free criticism of all theological claims.

Denying the historic doctrines of revelation and inspiration, free thinkers and agnostics like Robert Ingersol became popular. As ministers from modern seminaries took to the pulpits, churches began to neglect the gospel and to take up social and political issues. Many believers began to feel that they were orphans or sheep without a shepherd.

The quest for holiness

For the most part, believers were totally unprepared to counter the modernist inroad. The church had been the main instigator of learning and had no desire to be classed as ignorant and regressive. It was many years before liberalism was countered effectively.

In the meantime, there were new stirrings of interest in spiritual reality. Methodism, with its elaborate institutions and involvement in slavery and abolition issues, began to reach back to its roots. Concern over the change in Methodist doctrine and practice began to surface as, in 1843, the Wesleyan Methodist church was formed, mainly to restore Wesley's doctrine of holiness. The Methodist split between the North and the South over slavery in 1844 demanded reassessment and realignment not only of its structure but also of its doctrine.

Among the Methodists, Stephen Merritt created interest in the publication of *The Guide to Holiness* magazine. Purchased by Dr. and Mrs. Palmer in 1865, it reached a peak of forty thousand subscribers in 1870. Phoebe Palmer, an able orator and writer in New York City, reached many thousands. She emphasized that complete surrender to Christ would bring entire sanctification and Spirit baptism, and only those who were sanctified could escape losing their previous regeneration.

Mrs. Palmer was influenced by Wesley's associate, John Fletcher, who taught an experience of the soul in correspondence to what he called the dispensations of the Trinity. The Old Testament saints were under the dispensation of the Father, and the New Testament saints under Christ's dispensation could graduate to the dispensation of the Holy Spirit if they attained "the baptism of the Spirit" by entire sanctification.

Interdenominational Movements

Alongside the holiness interest fostered in Methodism, new interests began to unite evangelical believers of Congregational, Presbyterian, Reformed, Baptist, and other denominational backgrounds.

Revival and evangelism

In 1857, financial panic gripped America. In the North Dutch Church on Fulton Street in New York City, a revival broke out as prayer meetings were held during the noon hour for businessmen. As this revival spread elsewhere, it is estimated that a total of 750,000 people embraced Jesus Christ as Savior.

In this climate, in 1858, Dwight L. Moody of Chicago and John Wanamaker of Philadelphia started Sunday schools which grew into flourishing institutions. Evangelist and song leader teams gained wide attention. Moody-Sankey, Chapman-Alexander, and Whittle-Bliss were among the teams that traversed the country. Moody is believed to have addressed more than fifty million people and claimed 750,000 conversions.

Interdenominational organizations prospered. The Y.M.C.A., tract and Bible societies, temperance societies, rescue missions, and the Student Volunteer movement became part of the new spirit. In this type of background and environment The Christian and Missionary Alliance was born.

Missions and the Prophetic Conference movement

The revival and the anticipation of a new century created great interest in prophecy, particularly as promoted by the Brethren movement both in Europe and America. Premillennialism (the view that Christ will come before a thousand-year reign) began to be held as a point of orthodoxy. This was largely because postmillennialism was associated loosely with evolutionary theories that liberalism propounded, though it had been common in the Protestant churches in the early part of the century.

The premillennial doctrine taught that judgment would come to earth with the appearing of Christ before the ushering in of the millennium. The dispensational stress of the Brethren movement held that there would be a twofold coming of Christ with seven years of tribulation between the two comings.

The first prophetic conference was held in Chicago in 1878, followed by a series of conferences in the next twenty years. These meetings at first attracted great scholars and preachers of all denominations and became an evangelical spearhead of interdenominationalism that stirred a vision for missions. Many held that the Great Commission needed to be fulfilled before Christ would appear.

The absurdity of Christian competition in foreign countries developed interdenominational understanding and cooperation. One of the most far-reaching and effective organizations of this nature was the Student Volunteer movement established in 1886, designed to catch the imagination of Christian students throughout the world. John R. Mott became an outstanding leader in forming volunteer bands on campuses in preparation for foreign service. This gave rise to many faith missions with independent boards of government.

The Keswick movement

The beginning of the Keswick movement is traced to a

94

Philadelphia glass manufacturer, Robert Persall Smith, a Quaker and husband of Hannah Whitall Smith, noted author of the classic *The Christian's Secret of a Happy Life.* During a visit to London in 1873, Smith ministered among the wealthy of the Church of England at the Hampshire mansion in Broadlands. The Anglican vicar of Keswick became arrested with his teaching on "the sufficiency of Christ" and "rest in Him." He arranged a conference with Smith as speaker in 1875. When Smith suddenly canceled the engagement, D. L. Moody was invited in his place. This added great interest due to Moody's popularity. Moody had an experience of the Holy Spirit's infilling that had shaped his ministry.

Keswick became an interdenominational movement designed to promote practical holiness, but it had an emphasis different from that of Wesleyan perfectionism. In an introduction to *Keswick's Authentic Voice,* a book of Keswick addresses, Herbert T. Steven observes that *The Gospel Mystery of Sanctification* by Walter Marshall, the Puritan writer mentioned earlier in this chapter, contained everything that the Keswick emphasis taught. Another book mentioned is W. E. Boardman's *The Higher Christ Life.* Both had great influence on A. B. Simpson.

Keswick did not subscribe to any code of doctrine or polity and stressed the Spirit-filled life through the victorious Christ who by the vicarious atonement defeated self and sin in the life of a believer. Among Keswick supporters were Handley Moule, A. T. Pierson, F. B. Meyer, Andrew Murray, D. L. Moody, R. A. Torrey, S. D. Gordon, and G. Campbell Morgan, most of whom ministered one time or another at Simpson's Gospel Tabernacle in New York City. Keswick stood in the train of the Pietists and the Moravians but with added biblical grounding.

The National Holiness Association and Pentecostalism

The differences that existed initially between the holiness and Keswick movements arose from background, not from controversy. The inroads of militant liberalism generated a genuine thirst for Christian reality and became severely polarized from a belief in biblical authority. But hardening positions and widening differences also produced more factions.

Love for classical learning and the arts under the suffocating philosophies of humanistic idealism and Hegelianism became absorbed largely in materialism while evangelical forces were trying to recoup their losses. The quest for a revived church took many forms, but in the holiness movement it took a special turn of significance.

The National Holiness Association

The holiness movement became strongly identified by the National Holiness Association organized in 1867 in Philadelphia under the leadership of John S. Inskip. In a doctrinal statement adopted in 1885, it was stated that entire sanctification included the entire extinction of the carnal mind, the total eradication of the birth principle of sin, the communication of perfect love to the soul, and the abiding indwelling of the Holy Ghost.

By 1888, the Holiness Association listed 304 evangelists, and four publishing houses engaged in publishing holiness materials. By 1892, there were 41 holiness periodicals. As an independent organization of Methodist background, the National Holiness Association urged Methodist people to remain loyal to their churches and tried to defend itself against charges of "come-outism" being heard. But no uniform voice bridged communication.

With a strong lay orientation many self-styled revivalists emerged who had little training and who developed their own interpretations of holiness. In reaction to the Methodist ministerial loyalists and opposers of the second blessing, emotional patterns of thinking that centered on experience more than on biblical and theological thought became common. Extreme elements of various shades began to distort the image of the National Holiness Association.

Pentecostalism

Between 1895 and 1900, many denominations evolved,

particularly from among the four million of Methodist persuasion effected by the holiness movement. The Fire-Baptized Holiness Church under the leadership of Benjamin Irwin began in Iowa in 1895 and was organized into a denomination in 1898. Irwin had been a Baptist minister and an active member of the Iowa Holiness Association. Particularly from John Fletcher's writings he fastened upon the baptism of the Spirit and Fletcher's suggestion that many such baptisms might be necessary for the perfection of the believer.

Irwin taught that there was not only a second blessing of sanctification, which the holiness movement taught, but a third baptism of fire from the words of John the Baptist, *He will baptize you with the Holy Spirit and with fire* (Luke 3:16). Under Irwin's preaching emotional outbursts and falling into trances occurred which became associated with "the fire."

Having become unwelcome in the Iowa Holiness Association, Irwin founded the Iowa Fire-Baptized Holiness Association, which spread rapidly to ten states. This Association eventually gave birth to a number of different Pentecostal denominations.

The major thrust of pentecostalism with its "speaking in tongues" became widely known in 1906 as a result of "the Azusa Street Revival." This outbreak was under the influence of Charles F. Parham, who had been associated with Benjamin Irwin, and the preaching of a black student, W. J. Seymour.

Seymour had attended a Bible school conducted by Parham. It originated in Topeka, Kansas, where the phenomenon of speaking in tongues became prominent. It was said that a certain lady student had spoken in previously unknown languages and that in this "baptism" she was unable to speak English for three days. When asked to communicate in writing, she reportedly wrote in Chinese characters with which she had previously been unacquainted. In a revival that ensued in Parham's student body of forty, it was reported that in a gift of tongues twenty-one different languages were spoken.

The revival in the Topeka school stirred great interest, but nothing in comparison to the one on Azusa Street in Los Angeles where Seymour had gone to conduct a revival in a mission. Trainloads came from all over the country. They met scenes of men and women shouting, weeping, dancing, falling into trances, and speaking in tongues, with Seymour shouting defiance at anyone challenging the confusion.

Azusa recipients of blessing were looked upon with awe as apostles of Pentecost. For these speaking in tongues became the hallmark of a full and necessary experience of Christianity.

Those preoccupied with Pentecostal interests ignored the mainstream of evangelical thought and theology. The main interest of the Pentecostals for many years was to infiltrate the established churches, especially those affected by the holiness movement, with their view of Spirit-baptized Christianity. This caused difficult and embarrassing situations.

Bitter denunciations came from mainline denominational churches and even from valiant men in evangelical leadership. G. Campbell Morgan called the Pentecostal movement "the last vomit of Satan." R. A. Torrey claimed it was "emphatically not of God, and founded by a Sodomite"—reflecting Benjamin Irwin who started the "firebaptized" teaching and resigned his leadership in 1899 when he confessed open and gross sin. H. A. Ironside, for many years pastor of Moody Church, Chicago, described Pentecostal meetings as pandemoniums with exhibitions worthy of a madhouse causing a heavy toll of lunacy and infidelity.

The scorn experienced by Pentecostals became a unifying factor for them and peer pressure from evangelicals was interpreted as added incentive for their particular belief. Years of maturation and change in both Pentecostalism and evangelicalism as a whole have brought better understanding and relationship of common ground.

8

The Beginning of The Christian and Missionary Alliance

A. W. Tozer, in his biography of Albert B. Simpson, wrote:

His society (The Christian and Missionary Alliance) is himself grown large. It is the child of his heart, and it resembles its father as all good children should (*Wingspread: Albert B. Simpson—A Study in Spiritual Altitude;* Camp Hill, Pa.: Christian Publications, 1943, p. 102).

The history of The Christian and Missionary Alliance reveals the distinction of having been fostered and nurtured under the personal leadership of a particular man. Yet, no man lives or dies unto himself and seed is always the fruit of a family tree.

As the roots of a New Testament servant-people have their origin in the Old Testament, so, in part, the roots of the Alliance have their heritage in Simpson's ancestral environment.

The Scottish Heritage

After the French ceded Canada to England in 1763, a Scottish Presbyterian family, independent of spirit, looked for a fresh beginning in the New World. The William Simpson family with eight children emigrated from Morayshire, Scotland, and settled in Prince Edward Island in 1774.

The Presbyterian and Puritan influence

The Scottish Presbyterian strain in the New World had a unique heritage. Born out of a reform movement in England during the middle of the seventeenth century, it carried an unusual blend of character that cast a rugged, pervasive influence wherever it found root.

From the early fourteenth century, reform influence under leaders such as William of Occam, John Wycliff and the Lollards, William Tyndale, and John Knox rooted itself in the English soil. By 1540, a considerable number of lords, earls, barons, and lairds had accepted the new faith, and its espousal penetrated the learning centers of Oxford and Cambridge. When Queen Mary (1553-1558), a devout Catholic, sought to repeal the reforming acts of Henry VIII and Edward VI, a power struggle with severe persecution ensued. As a result, many English Protestants fled into exile, to either Scotland or the Continent.

Puritan preaching had a powerful effect in Scotland. With the accession of Mary Stuart (1561-1567) to the throne in Scotland, a situation similar to that in England developed. Religious persecution climaxed with military conflict. Finally, under the leadership of John Knox, this was resolved through a covenant giving the church a Presbyterian form of government. Scottish Presbyterianism was steeped in the Bible and shaped by Calvinist doctrine and discipline. Its preaching was marked by a plain style, cogent and terse, yet deeply spiritual.

Presbyterian preaching strongly emphasized "the whole counsel of God" and the sovereignty of God. Presbyterianism held that there were two kings and two kingdoms in Scotland. While the church was ruled by a changeable civil government, there was an unchangeable sovereign God and kingdom that ruled the world by divine providence. Further, it taught plainly that man was lost in depravity and needed spiritual enlightenment and transformation through the gospel and that character in life and work was the proof of the gospel and its preaching.

The Simpson parentage

Albert Simpson's father stood staunchly in the Presbyterian succession of life, spirit, and high tradition. He was a good elder of the old school, believing his children should be grounded in the Shorter Catechism and all the principles of an ordered Presbyterian household. As an officer in the church he was respected for his knowledge of the Scriptures, his sound judgment, consistent life, and strong practical sense. Rising long before daylight, he would have his morning devotions by a lighted candle. In the family library were books of Puritan and Pietistic authorship. When the family was unable to attend services in the church nine miles from their home in Chatham, Ontario, worship services were conducted in the home.

Albert's mother, Jane Clark before her marriage, also was of Scottish ancestry. Her father had been a member of the legislature and her brother William was elected to his father's seat at his death and continued in office until he was eighty years old. Mrs. Simpson often told her children stories she had heard from her maternal Grandmother McEwan of the persecutions suffered during the Scottish Reformation. Widely known and greatly respected in her family tradition, Albert's mother had a love for literature and a refinement in Christian principles that served as a balance to the sternness of Albert's father.

The Birth and Early Ministry of the Founder

Through all of biblical and church history, God has used Spirit-endowed men to direct His people in carrying out His redemptive plan. Paul exhorted the Corinthian church to eagerly desire the greater gifts (1 Cor. 12:31). The book of Acts leaves little doubt concerning who had the greater gifts —for the most part those persons who were used of God in founding and establishing the church. Albert Simpson was one of those with the greater gifts.

The birth of Albert B. Simpson
On December 15, 1843, in a modest home on Prince Edward Island, Canada, Albert B. Simpson was born. His

mother prayed that he might become a minister or a missionary "if the Lord so wills and he lives to grow up and is so inclined." That under the providence of God he would become both bears testimony of a God who does more than we can ask or think. Albert was baptized as an infant in the Presbyterian church by Rev. John Geddie, the apostle to Aneityum in the South Sea Islands. He was three when the family moved to Chatham. At the age of fourteen, young Albert learned from his father that his older brother could draw on family funds to go to college. He, the younger son, would be expected to remain at home and work on the farm. This almost crushed him, for from the age of ten Albert had carried a secret desire to become a minister. After a hard emotional struggle, he made his desire known to his father. Although his physical frame was none too robust, he promised to earn his way for his education if permission would be granted. His father made a solemn evaluation and in his Calvinistic belief in foreordination he accepted this as the will of God.

Albert, however, had not yet found his peace with God. This came at the age of fifteen during a trial of sickness that threatened his life. His full assurance of salvation came through the reading of Walter Marshall's *The Gospel Mystery of Sanctification.*

After being graduated from high school at the age of sixteen, Albert taught school. During this time he read Phillip Doddridge's *Rise and Progress of Religion in the Soul* and made a "solemn covenant" of self-dedication to God. A concluding portion of this lengthy document read:

"I have now, O Lord, as Thou hast said in Thy Word, covenanted with Thee, not for worldly honors or fame but for everlasting life, and I know that Thou art true and shalt never break Thy holy Word. Give to me now all the blessings of the New Covenant and especially the Holy Spirit in great abundance, which is the earnest of my inheritance until the redemption of the purchased possession. May a double portion of Thy Spirit rest upon me, and then I shall go and proclaim to transgressors Thy ways and Thy laws to the people. Sanctify me wholly and make me fit for heaven. Give me all spiritual blessing in heavenly places in Christ Jesus.

"I am now a soldier of the cross and a follower of the Lamb, and my motto from henceforth is 'I have one King, even Jesus.' Support and strengthen me, O my Captain, and be mine forever" (as quoted by A. E. Thompson, *A. B. Simpson: His Life and Work;* Camp Hill, Pa.: Christian Publications, 1960, p. 22).

Pastor at Hamilton (1865-1873)

When he was eighteen, Albert entered Knox College, Toronto, in preparation for the ministry. Even as a student he proved himself an able pulpiteer. Three months after graduation he was ordained to the Presbyterian ministry and became pastor of Knox Church in Hamilton, Ontario. The next day he married Margaret Henry of Toronto whom he had courted for three years.

Simpson ministered in Hamilton for eight years and received 750 members. His Sunday sermons were often printed in the local newspaper. His travels took him once to Europe. Even into his late years, he was called back periodically to this first pastorate on a special occasion.

Pastor at Louisville (1873-1879)

Simpson's call to the Chestnut Street Presbyterian Church in Louisville, Kentucky, came about through an earlier visit to New York to attend a conference. The pastor at the Thirteenth Street Presbyterian Church, Dr. Burchard, invited Simpson to preach in his Sunday services and delegates from Louisville heard him preach. Later, the Louisville congregation invited him to become their pastor. After six years there, the call to become pastor of the Thirteenth Street church in New York was received.

Soon after becoming the pastor in Louisville, Simpson read W. E. Boardman's book, *The Higher Christian Life,* was filled with the Spirit, and in many ways began a new life. He had prayed long and often concerning his carnal ways, wanted to be "sanctified," and sometimes thought he was. In desperation he had tried to hold on to an experience, until the realization finally came that sanctification is Christ himself indwelling the believer's life through the Holy Spirit. He later stated that "what men and women need to know today is not sanctification as a state but Christ as a living Person" (Thompson, p. 68). He wrote:

"I look back with unutterable gratitude to the lonely and sorrowful night when, mistaken in many things and imperfect in all, and not knowing but that it would be death in the most literal sense before the morning light, my heart's full consecration was made, and with unreserved surrender I first could say,

Jesus, I my cross have taken,
All to leave and follow Thee;
Destitute, despised, forsaken,
Thou from hence my All shall be."
(Thompson, p. 65)

To Simpson this was a crisis experience. It was a transaction of claiming by faith the full inheritance of the gospel. His experience ignited a new flame in his heart and influenced him to request the other city pastors to join him in conducting an evangelistic campaign. They agreed and invited the newly formed team of Major D. W. Whittle and P. P. Bliss to Louisville. Dr. Simpson discovered that both of these men were experiencing the Spirit-filled life. They were particularly helpful to him at that point in his ministry.

For these evangelistic meetings, the Public Library Hall had been rented, and because of the manner as well as the results of the campaign, the whole course and concept of Simpson's ministry began to change. He came to see evangelistic outreach as a basic priority which he had previously given to parish care. He recognized that the power of God through evangelistic preaching could reach multitudes totally neglected by denominational, pew-rent churches.

After the Whittle-Bliss campaign, Simpson moved his Sunday evening services to the Library Hall, where hundreds were converted. Later, the Chestnut Street church built the beautiful Broadway Tabernacle seating about two thousand persons, and where pew rents were eliminated.

The vision of reaching people carried Simpson beyond Louisville. While a missionary board had been formed by the Presbyterians in 1837 and missionaries had been sent to India, Africa, and China, Simpson began to sense the fact that the abilities of the churches for aggressive evangelism were not being fully utilized. It seemed to him that the *go* and *woe* of Christian missions were seemingly mired in the web of social and secular concerns that looked toward humanistic solutions for the ills of the world rather than to the power of the gospel. It was in Louisville that Simpson first began to formulate in his own mind the idea of publishing a missionary periodical that might alter the situation.

When the pastoral call came from the Thirteenth Street church, Simpson felt that New York City was the better place to launch his illustrated missionary magazine. Missionary information would be closer at hand and missionaries often passed through the port of New York. He wanted his magazine to cross denominational lines and trusted that it would ignite the whole church to the limits of missionary potential.

The dream was being realized—for in February of 1880, Simpson published in New York the first issue of *The Gospel in All Lands.*

Pastor at New York City (1879-1881)

The well-known Thirteenth Street church took on new life upon the arrival of the new pastor, but Simpson proved to be far ahead of the congregation in his burden to reach the city. The parish family consisted largely of upper middle-class families, who considered it their priority to bring in new members of their own social status. Pews were rented to members as the way to meet church expenses. Later, when Simpson asked the church session for permission to bring more than a hundred of his converts from the Italian quarter into membership, his request was denied.

The growing realization that the Thirteenth Street church would not serve as a base for evangelistic outreach crushed the pastor's aspirations. Always weak physically, the burden and frustrations of his ministry contributed to serious breaks in his health. He was forced to take several protracted vacations, and his doctors finally pronounced that if he did not close out his ministry he would live for only a few months.

One of his vacations had taken Simpson to Old Orchard, Maine, a famous summer resort as well as a campmeeting site. In the desperate situation with his health, he returned to Old Orchard praying for the solution to his problems.

When he arrived at the campgrounds, he found that Dr. Cullis, a Boston medical doctor, was conducting a series of meetings with particular emphasis upon his own conviction of the validity of the doctrine of divine healing as well as the similar convictions held by such men as Dr. A. J. Gordon of Boston, W. E. Boardman, then living in England, and Pastor Blumhardt of Germany. Probably their writings had come to Simpson's attention. He was driven to his Bible and, after careful study, became convinced within himself that the living Christ had made provision for the healing of the physical body as well as for the soul.

Going alone into a pine grove along the coast of Maine, Simpson committed his entire physical infirmity to the Lord. The next day he boarded a train with his family to go to Intervale, New Hampshire, where they worshiped on Sunday.

On Monday morning, he joined a hiking party preparing to climb nearby Mount Kearsage, an altitude of about three thousand feet. When he reached the pinnacle, faith had gained the victory and he realized a different life flowing from the power of the indwelling Christ. From that time, he drew his physical and mental energies from the Lord.

Upon his return to New York, Simpson felt a strong leading to reach out to the neglected people of New York City. He had also become convinced that baptism by immersion is the biblical mode and quietly asked to be baptized in a small Baptist church in the city. Having reached this conviction, he knew that it could become a source of embarrassment both for himself and for the Presbytery. This situation was just another reason to follow the conviction of his heart to cut all official ties with his church and launch out in faith to minister to the masses in the city. His resignation from the Thirteenth Street church was effective in November, 1881.

The Birth of The Christian and Missionary Alliance

Through the New York newspapers, Simpson announced

that he would conduct Sunday afternoon meetings in Cale-donia Hall near Eighth Avenue. In his farewell sermon in the Presbyterian church, he had cautioned the members not to follow him, but to remain loyal to their church.

His first message as an independent preacher dealt with the spiritual needs as he saw them in New York City. He in-vited those who were in the Sunday afternoon meeting to re-main for a second session if they were interested in prayer and consultation on ways to evangelize the needy. Only seven persons responded, one of whom was the ex-drunkard, Josephus Pulis.

During the next eight years, the group expanded to well over a thousand persons. The meetings were held in such places as Academy of Music, Steinway Hall, Grand Opera Hall, a tent, an armory expanded into a theater, a massive church building, and ultimately Madison Square Garden, then known as the Hippodrome. Simpson and his growing group were attempting something for God for which there was no precedent at the time.

The New York Tabernacle

Sunday afternoon and evening services continued. In February 1882, a group of thirty-five adherents went to Simpson's home and joined in the organization of a church based on a simple constitution. Dr. Simpson wrote of this move:

Its method of church government is exceedingly sim-ple, being chiefly congregational with the addition of a board of elders who in conjunction with the pastors, ex-ercise the spiritual oversight of the Church (*The Story of the C. & M. A.;* New York: Christian Alliance Pub-lishing, 1900, p. 20).

The constitution and bylaws read:

1. The Word of God alone shall be the rule of doctrine, practice and discipline in this church; it being always understood that we receive it as the inspired Word of God, and the only divine rule of faith and conduct.

2. That we recognize and receive the Lord Jesus Christ as the true and divine Son of the living God, the only Head of the Church and our only Saviour, and

Master; and the Holy Spirit in His divine personality as the only source and channel of all true spiritual life and power.

3.   That we recognize in Christian fellowship and affection the one Church of God, consisting of all true believers of whatever name, and that we desire to stand in Christian communion with every organization of evangelical Christians who hold and practice the truth as it is in Jesus, and are organized and constituted in accordance with the Word of God, for the work of the Gospel.

4.   While we recognize it as our high calling, in connection with every true church of Christ, to worship and witness for God and His truth, and to cherish, nurture and edify His children, and to build up His kingdom; yet it will ever be recognized as the specific mission of this church to promote the work of evangelization among the neglected classes at home and abroad, as God may enable us in every part of the world.

5.   The profession of living faith in the Lord Jesus Christ, a sincere purpose to live according to His will and for His glory; and the evidence of a consistent moral and Christian character and life, will be the only conditions of membership in this church.

6.   New members will be received at the regular monthly business meeting on the recommendation of the Pastor and Elders, on their public confession of faith and the vote of the members.

7.   The ordinance of baptism will be administered on profession of faith and ordinarily by immersion. Persons who have been baptized otherwise, or in infancy, will be received if they are satisfied with their own baptism. Parents will have the privilege of presenting their infant children in the house of God for public consecration to God.

8.   The Lord's Supper will be administered not less frequently than once every month on the second Lord's day of the month.

It is easy to overlook the distinct feature of this constitution. Here is the forthright declaration of the place of God's

Word in the church, the recognition of Christ as the only head, the Holy Spirit as the only source and channel of true spiritual life and power, and the recognition of the organized, visible, local church in communion with the universal church.

Tozer wrote of this development: "A. B. Simpson was in his glory. He was seeing Christian democracy at its simple best. His members came from every level of human society from the gutter to the penthouse. . . . It was a free Church in the fullest sense of the Word" (*Wingspread*, p. 89).

From this church other projects evolved with phenomenal rapidity and success. The New York Missionary Training College was founded in October 1882, Simpson having conducted training classes for church workers in 1881. The training college served as a center for missionary workers, particularly, most of them recruited through Simpson's preaching.

Simpson also began a publishing business in January 1883, from which came the periodical, *The Word, Work, and World,* the forerunner of *The Alliance Witness.* In 1883, Simpson also opened a home for people desiring spiritual help and counsel and for those needing physical healing. The number of people requesting such help so increased that a larger facility was necessary. The Berachah Home, as it was known, was moved to Nyack in 1897. Early in Simpson's ministry, several rescue missions were opened; an orphanage was started at College Point on Long Island, and transferred to Nyack. The training institute was moved to Nyack in 1897.

*The Christian Alliance and The Evangelical
Missionary Alliance*

Simpson's ministries had begun to reach out to larger cities throughout the United States and in eastern Canada, and spiritually hungry people were responding with a desire to become a part of this kind of fellowship and work. In August 1887 at Old Orchard, Maine, the work that was centered in the New York Gospel Tabernacle was expanded into two segments, The Christian Alliance and The Evangelical Missionary Alliance, both distinct from the Tabernacle in administrative function.

Simpson said of this new enterprise:

"No new society should be organized to do what is already being done by some other society. If there is some new principle to be worked out, some new method to be proved, some new agency to be employed, or some wholly unoccupied region to be reached, it is all right to attempt it, provided the movement is wisely planned and carried out by experienced and consecrated men. But simply to repeat what is being done somewhere else, or to start a new society because Hudson Taylor, Dr. Guinness, Andrew Murray, or somebody else has started a society, will simply prove like the echo of the parrot's voice as it tries to repeat the empty sound that has fallen upon its ear" (Thompson, pp. 125-6).

The Christian Alliance, according to the platform adopted, was designed to be an organization to which people of various evangelical churches could belong. Simpson frequently wrote editorials advising that the Alliance was not designed to become a new church. Members of these Alliance branches were to be soundly evangelical. There was interest in their moral and spiritual character as well as in their financial support.

Basic evangelical orthodoxy was subscribed to in a simple, direct statement, incorporating a firm belief in the verbal inspiration of the Holy Scriptures, the doctrine of the Trinity, the atoning sacrifice of the Lord Jesus Christ, and the necessity of a regenerating and sanctifying work of the Holy Spirit.

The Alliance was not to be an ecclesiastical body, not because Simpson and others did not believe in the church, for the New York Gospel Tabernacle itself had been organized as a church. But Simpson wanted members of the Alliance to recognize the Four-fold Gospel—Christ Our Savior, Sanctifier, Healer, and Coming King—and to find their bond of unity and fellowship in this expressed truth.

Also, members of the Christian Alliance were urged to remain loyal as members of evangelical churches and to have meetings that would inspire missionary prayer and fellowship in the work of The Missionary Alliance. The work of the second organization was to administer recruiting, training, and sending of missionaries.

Simpson called this "simply a fraternal union of consecrated believers in connection with the various evangelical churches" (Thompson, p. 129). The "connection" referred to was the initial membership of those who belonged to evangelical churches and also joined The Evangelical Alliance. The regular church was needed. It was to be fully recognized as the backbone of the Alliance, but a new loyalty was to be superimposed without interference in the program and work of the local church!

These auxiliary groups were called Alliance branches, not churches. The leaders were superintendents, not pastors; its interrelationship was called a fraternal union, not a denomination. Branches often were mistaken for rescue missions and the missionary cause was often mistaken for an independent faith mission.

As for the Gospel Tabernacle, its membership had grown from 35 to 219 within a year after its organization. The Sunday evening services were attracting about 700 people. Evangelistic services and other meetings were held during the week. In the summer months, Simpson pitched large tents on vacant lots to reach the lost and continued to train lay members to minister in missions, in hospitals, and in jails. One of the missions was opened particularly to minister to the large number of sailors found in New York.

Tozer wrote:

Several organizations were formed from the teeming life of the Tabernacle fellowship, each with a specific object in view and with a particular function to perform. For instance there were no less than six young people's societies, all going full blast at one and the same time! There was no overlapping. They knew what they were called to do, and they did it with enthusiasm (*Wingspread*, p. 93).

Pastor Simpson had a motto for the church: "A work for everyone and everyone at work."

Approximately seventeen years after the church had begun with thirty-five members, it had grown to more than fourteen hundred.

The Christian and Missionary Alliance

Facts are far too cold and hard to use to evaluate what was happening. It was apparent that the teaching of the imminent return of Christ had become a major motivation in Alliance work and fellowship. The supreme duty was to take the gospel to those neglected places where the message of Christ had not yet penetrated. At the great summer missionary conventions, the challenge of missions moved the audiences not only to give their money but also their gold rings, jewelry, and watches in order to facilitate the work.

Humble tabernacles became centers for recruiting converts for the missionary cause. Spiritual gifts became pronounced as teaching on the Holy Spirit and divine healing was emphasized. Missionaries, evangelists, and gospel singing fired the hearts of the masses. Unusual answers to prayer and miracles occurred regularly. This was considered the apostolic church revived. The environment of expediency and sacrificial giving was part of the blessing.

On the cold and hard side, expediency was sacrificing principle in many areas of the work. Inadequate attention was given to the local church in its need for a settled, adequate teaching ministry that would cause members to pool their gifts to edify the church indigenously and contribute to the community.

Interdenominationalism became an excuse for ignoring aspects of individual, particular responsibility in local church situations, though this was not the founder's intention. The idealized spiritual church replaced the local church where convenient, and some teachings heard in less cultivated areas stressed that the local church was considered outmoded by new styles of evangelical fellowship.

In one decade, in order to facilitate and coordinate the work that had developed, the two organizations, The Christian Alliance and The Evangelical Missionary Alliance, were formed into what is now known as The Christian and Missionary Alliance. As newly formed Alliance branches gained converts and as people came who were dissatisfied with their own churches, they were not being directed to seek evangelical churches. The superintendents of the branches, urged to live by faith and freewill offerings, needed support and workers to build and contribute for a larger ministry.

In the larger metropolitan centers where conventions had found a large following, prototypes of the Gospel Tabernacle gradually became centers of strong support for the Alli nce missionary cause. In the weaker areas, Alliance branches resembled rescue missions or Salvation Army halls. Too often, Alliance branches became struggling centers of gospel activity trying to do the work of a local church while disclaiming to be one.

Thus, a strange thing was happening. A "new agency"— not an acknowledged church—was striving to give birth overseas to free churches of a biblical nature. Although the society continued to train home workers, superintendents, city missionaries, and rescue mission workers, the focus was on missions. This was the primary purpose of the society from the beginning.

Thus begins the story of The Christian and Missionary Alliance.

UNDERSTANDING THE CHRISTIAN AND MISSIONARY ALLIANCE IN THE TWENTIETH CENTURY

Christianity in our day still has important decisions to make relative to its responsibilities throughout the world. It is safe to say that if Christianity should elect to assume the "static" position, digging in only to protect the status quo, it cannot survive.

Any study of the past growth and influence of Christianity will reveal a phenomenon that cannot be denied—opposition, persecution and martyrdom have never been able to blunt the cutting edge of Christian evangelism.

At the close of the New Testament canon, Christian believers numbered perhaps 500,000 in a world population of 250 million (a ratio of 1 to 500). Historians have indicated that by A.D. 1500, the ratio of Christian believers in the world population had changed drastically to about 1 to 30. It has now been indicated that if contemporary trends continue into the twenty-first century, it is possible that there will be one professing Christian for every four persons in the world at that time.

How the church views itself and its responsibility in today's context is deeply significant. Everything has been placed under Christ's feet and He has been appointed *head over everything for the church, . . .* (Eph. 1:22).

The Christian and Missionary Alliance at its beginning viewed itself as a new agency with new principles to be worked out and new methods to be applied. Much has happened in this century; much is changing. Do we discern these changes as occurring under God's providence? Do they measure up to the scriptural church pattern? If continued guidance is to be realized with faith, we must be honest in seeking the answers to these questions.

9

The Christian and Missionary Alliance As an Interdenominational Society

The design of The Christian and Missionary Alliance to function as an evangelizing movement in cooperation with existing churches was not without precedent in ongoing church history.

In the seventeenth century, the Pietist movement within the Lutheran church organized the Halle-Danish Mission that sent sixty missionaries to the fields and emphasized conversion and sanctification.

The Moravians, in perpetuating the Pietist movement, organized societies designed to function as an international association for missionary endeavor and to include true believers of various denominational churches. Sending out hundreds of missionaries, the Moravians became an effective modern-day missionary force.

In the nineteenth century, while in the Church of England, John Wesley began Methodist societies through which to spread the doctrine of holiness among all denominations. Both the Moravians and Methodists, however, eventually became denominational churches.

The Christian and Missionary Alliance, developing as an interdenominational society in the early twentieth century when parachurch organizations had a high credibility, soon discovered a variety of unexpected pressures as it sought to establish its identity.

Having begun as the New York Gospel Tabernacle, an independent church, the Alliance has a distinction few people understand fully. Between 1900 and the year of Simpson's death, 1919, many events and decisions served in shaping and molding its distinctive character.

The Christian and Missionary Alliance: Church or Parachurch? (1900-1919)

Referring to beginnings of "this special work," Simpson wrote in an early issue of *The Word, Work and World:*
At first there was no formal organization, but as Christians began to unite in the work and converts to need a church home, it became manifest that God was calling the brethren thus associated to organize a Christian church for this special work according to the principles and example of His Word (as quoted by Thompson, p. 93).
Simpson's enthusiasm and vision for the church was plainly expressed when he said:
"My plan and idea of a church are those which are exemplified in the great London churches of Newman Hall and of Spurgeon, comprising thousands of members of no particular class, but of the rich and poor side by side" (Thompson, p. 94).

The church: a New Testament pattern
There is evidence that Simpson and his followers recognized the church as having a biblical base for carrying out God's redemptive purpose in the world. The Evangelical Missionary Alliance was organized in 1887, with its constitution stating this purpose:
It will leave each church established on the foreign field free to organize and administer its affairs as it may choose, provided that such method be scriptural in its essential features (Thompson, p. 131).
This was a statement based on the belief that an indigenous church was essential in all lands as an established root of

the gospel.

George P. Pardington, early an instructor in theology at Nyack Missionary Training Institute, consistently used New Testament examples in teaching that local churches are made up of born-again believers voluntarily joined together, among whom the Word of God is preached, discipline is administered, and the ordinances observed. He pointed to the flexibility in church government. The form was more congregational than episcopal or presbyterian, since local churches in the New Testament exercised authority to elect their own leaders and to discipline and exclude members. In a sense, each church had the power to determine all matters not already determined by the Scriptures.

Beyond this, however, there evidently was a wider form than the local church, for congregations, in the plural, were grouped within a country and a council of churches was held at Jerusalem (theology notes published posthumously as *Outline Studies in Christian Doctrine*).

These principles and practices of the local churches, however, were not necessarily those of The Christian and Missionary Alliance branches, which were strictly parachurch.

In one of Simpson's sermons, he pointed out the special and unique ministry which related certain movements to the churches:

The work of the China Inland Mission, the rise of The Christian and Missionary Alliance, and the Student Volunteers, give some intimation of what such a movement might be under the direction of the Holy Ghost if the church of Christ were only aroused to a full realization of the need of the world, the opportunities of the time, and the urgency of the call. It is just such a movement as this that the church of Christ and the heathen world need. Nothing short of it can meet the awful destitution of the world and the apathy, indifference and selfishness of the church. It is not too much to say that the whole world might be occupied in half a generation and the Lord's coming hastened in our time.... It would usher in an era of glory and spiritual quickening such as the church has not witnessed since the days of Paul. . . . Oh, for a missionary trust, a combination of idle capital and the elevated minds and hearts of the church of God to accomplish in a prodigious enterprise as much for God as mammon is doing in a thousand directions for selfishness and pleasure! (*The Challenge of Missions*, pp. 21-22)

Missionary conventions, which began in the Gospel Tabernacle in New York City in 1884, spread rapidly with great blessing to Brooklyn, Buffalo, Philadelphia, Pittsburgh, Chicago, and Detroit. To serve the established church in its ministry of missions, however, The Christian and Missionary Alliance would become an interdenominational agency. A number of factors explain why the main work of The Christian and Missionary Alliance was to advance by cooperative effort in a worldwide missionary task that would bless and encourage all evangelical churches:

1. A number of growing movements—holiness, Pentecostal, independent church, fundamentalist—were capitalizing on the divisions taking place in established churches because of the inroads of liberalism and doctrinal disputation. Many denominations that emerged at the turn of the century were also marked by extremism of various kinds.

It was against this kind of backdrop that The Christian and Missionary Alliance felt its call to helpful evangelistic and deeper life ministries, hopefully moving toward a true evangelical ecumenicity that should mark the body of Christ.

2. The principles and methods adopted by The Christian and Missionary Alliance served the church uniquely in its missionary outreach, particularly those congregations which had no affiliation with any denominational or independent missionary board. It was only proper that these supporting segments of the missionary cause should have a voice in the policies and methods being adopted overseas and that they should display the same convictions of message, vision, and commitment as the missionaries who represented them.

3. By setting forth The Christian and Missionary Alliance as an interdenominational society, clearly designed not to infringe on the churches, a momentum of

cooperation and good will could be established.

This would demonstrate a transparency of motives and a force of conviction to all evangelical churches and groups. With a simple but clear focus on Christ's sufficiency for all men, cooperating churches could agree to disagree on minor points of doctrine where basic orthodoxy and soundness were not involved.

4.   The emphasis upon the biblical promises of Christ's Second Coming to earth and their relationship to the importance of carrying out the Great Commission added much in the continuing acceptance of The Christian and Missionary Alliance and its ministries as a parachurch organization.

These were some of the major factors apparent to the earliest leaders of the movement as decisions were made for ministries and mission. To the end of his life, Dr. Simpson believed that his vision was being vindicated and that in his generation the gospel could be taken to every tongue, tribe, and nation. The church was the biblical norm and base for this potential, and The Christian and Missionary Alliance was simply an agency to aid the church in reaching this potential. In Simpson's view, the church was God's means of accomplishing the task, but the situation and climate plus the emergency of the hour could not allow sectarianism or narrow interests to prevail.

The Society: a unique parachurch agency

It should be repeated that the Alliance clearly was not a dissenting, disgruntled group of people made up of those who had left divided churches. The Society had begun as a byproduct of the great Bible and deeper life conventions and from the desire of many persons from various evangelical churches to get into the missionary work with a full life commitment.

The Christian and Missionary Alliance was neither an antidenominational nor an independent church movement. The influence of the holiness movement and of the independent tabernacle and Bible church movements became widespread in the early 1900s, bringing about a reaction to institutionalism and denominationalism.

Among the reactions often heard was this: doctrinal standards and creeds serve only to keep people apart, but a Christianity without denominations would unite all Christians in fellowship. This individualistic sectarianism soon became vulnerable to extreme views, and emphasis on experience without due regard for scriptural truth led to much that was simply shallow and sensational.

Simpson and other Alliance leaders made it plain that undisciplined and unsettled elements would not be allowed to dominate the constituency. In May 1906, a Prayer Conference on Alliance Truth and Testimony was held to clarify and unify doctrinal positions, particularly in regard to sanctification. The Society indicated it would continue as an interdenominational force. Erratic and inconsistent tactics of revivalism without adequate teaching and identification in fellowship were discouraged.

Another kind of pressure developed as denominational church members dissatisfied with the spiritual life in their own churches were attracted to fellowship in Alliance branches. When testimonies of conversion and spiritual blessing were given in their churches, they found they were no longer welcome. This was reflected in an *Alliance Weekly* article in 1912:

> While the Alliance movement to a certain extent is unavoidably a self-contained organization and requires a sufficient amount of executive machinery to hold it together and make it effective, yet we must never forget that it has a certain interdenominational message for the Christian church today and that this ministry must not be clouded by any narrow sectarian tendencies. . . . There are cases continually arising where it is necessary to provide special and permanent religious privileges for little bands of Christian disciples who have either been converted in some evangelistic movement or pushed out of their churches by false teaching and harsh pressure and prejudice. Yet these local and independent congregations should never be considered as Alliance churches in any technical sense, but simply independent churches which God Himself has specially raised up "through the present distress"

and over which we exercise for the time a certain spiritual oversight.

In 1914, G. P. Pardington explained the emergence and relationship of independent churches:

In cities and villages, in many instances, it was not a happy arrangement to send our converts to the churches for baptism. Indeed, our people were often made to feel that not only for the ordinance of baptism but also for the observance of the Lord's Supper they were not welcome in the churches. In these circumstances the Board considered it wise, where the conditions were ripe and the need was urgent, to encourage the branches to effect a simple New Testament church organization. In a number of places this was done.

In country areas, the situation was somewhat different. In many sparsely settled districts Christians were found without church homes and children without Sunday school privileges. In such places Sunday schools were organized and regular Sunday services established. Out of these conditions, in some instances, churches grew up. They became, in fact, a necessity; for the field was unoccupied, none of the evangelical denominations ministering to the spiritual destitution of the people.

There are today throughout the entire country about fifty independent Full Gospel churches in association with the Alliance. These churches, it must be clearly understood, are not Alliance churches. There is, in fact, no such thing as an Alliance church. Nor indeed can there be, for The Christian and Missionary Alliance is not a denominational body nor in any wise a sectarian movement (*Twenty-five Wonderful Years*, pp. 92-94).

Unable to function as a New Testament church, the Alliance found expansion of the home base increasingly difficult. Ostensibly, branches were not to be established by the making of converts. These were to be conserved in churches before becoming a part of the branch.

The Christian and Missionary Alliance was not a fundamentalist movement. In 1909, ten small booklets were printed and widely distributed under the general title of "The

Fundamentals." These upheld unreservedly five points of doctrine commonly held by evangelical churches: the inerrancy of Scripture, the virgin birth of Christ, Christ's physical Resurrection, the substitutionary Atonement, and the imminent and physical return of Christ. With the exception of the imminent return of Christ, the Presbyterian General Assembly affirmed these points as late as 1923.

In 1919, the Christian Fundamentals Association was organized in America and a series of conventions alerted people to what was happening. Griffith Thomas of England took the lead to organize a similar association internationally. He was supported by scholars like James Orr and G. Campbell Morgan. The issues took on larger proportions when a young science teacher, John T. Scopes, contravened a state law prohibiting the teaching of evolution in the schools in Dayton, Tennessee. William Jennings Bryan and Clarence Darrow locked horns as opposing lawyers.

While fundamentalists continued to penetrate the major denominations, causing severe divisions in many cases, The Christian and Missionary Alliance was intent on keeping to its original design—to create a fraternal fellowship of evangelical churches, emphasizing a translation of evangelical theology into spiritual life, aiding in promotion of overseas missions. In his presidential report to Council, Simpson reminded the constituency that it did not comprise a "comeout" movement. Although continuing to uphold the five principal points of fundamentalism, the Alliance never became a declared part of the fundamentalist movement.

Faithful exposition of the Scriptures and emphasis upon the all-sufficient Savior attracted many who had become frustrated with controversy. Fundamental theology was never threatened in any way within the Alliance movement.

The Christian and Missionary Alliance was not a tongues movement. The Pentecostal movement made its debut into American religious life at the beginning of the twentieth century. Doctrinally, the Pentecostal groups were sympathetic to the deeper life teaching of A. B. Simpson but its adherents held one distinguishing tenet that he firmly rejected—that the baptism of the Spirit must always be accompanied by the physical manifestation of supernatural

126

tongues. This belief became so overpowering that it absorbed most of their interests and separated them from many other evangelical groups.

Various Pentecostal leaders frequently came to the Gospel Tabernacle in the early expansion years of their movement. To know more about them, A.B. Simpson sent Dr. Henry Wilson, his associate and field supervisor, to Alliance, Ohio to observe and report. His conclusion was: "I am not able to approve the movement, though I am willing to concede that there is probably something of God in it somewhere."

After much prayer, Simpson published a statement in 1906 that was kind but firm. He made it plain that the gifts of the Spirit, especially that of tongues, were not to be confused with the filling of the Spirit and that a truly sanctified life was best demonstrated by the fruits of the Spirit.

Some who were leaders in the Alliance, both men and women, and a number of congregations withdrew from the Society. Their action was a severe blow to Simpson personally, but he stood upon the position that The Christian and Missionary Alliance was not to be part of the tongues movement.

The Christian and Missionary Alliance was not a healing movement. Simpson had personally experienced reality in physical healing and had vowed before God that he would teach its truth. He regarded the truth of divine healing as a a sacred trust and would not allow it to become a professional business or a public parade. He did not like the terms "faith healing" or "faith cure," but used "divine healing" instead because physical healing must come from God alone.

Every Friday afternoon, Simpson conducted a consecration and healing service. He and others prayed with seekers, and many persons were healed. This practice continued without interruption for about thirty-eight years, 1882 to 1919. The meetings were based on Bible study, out of which Simpson finally published the volume, *The Lord for the Body*. At these meetings, many persons testified to God's healing power, and prayer requests for healing came from around the world. For those attending the meetings and requesting their help, the leaders prayed, anointing them with oil in keeping with James 5:14-16. Simpson would not keep statistics, but stated that hundreds who gathered for the Friday meetings were healed and the total would reach into the thousands (*The Gospel of Healing*, p. 185).

Simpson was keenly aware that problems surrounded the subject of divine healing. In spite of his own remarkable deliverance and the healing shortly thereafter of his daughter, sick with diptheria, he stated that for several years he preached the gospel in evangelistic services without a single reference to bodily healing. He did not want to prejudice his listeners with "side issues." He revealed his personal convictions and attitudes quite frankly:

> I have never allowed anyone to look to me as a healer, and have had no liberty to pray for others while they placed the least trust in either me or my prayers, or aught but the merits, promises and intercessions of Christ alone.
>
> My most important work has usually been to get myself and my shadow out of people's way, and to set Jesus fully in their view. . . . I have never felt called to urge anyone to accept divine healing. I have found it better to present the truth and let God lead them. . . . I have never felt that divine healing should be regarded as the gospel. It is part of it, but we labor much more assiduously for the salvation and sanctification of the souls of men (*The Gospel of Healing*, pp. 180, 183-184).

Simpson's emphasis on healing was kept in appropriate bounds. He did all that he could to keep the doctrine of healing from causing division among Christian brethren. He refused to debate the doctrine publicly and would not share a platform with those who wished to do so. Though not essential to orthodoxy, healing was presented as a magnificent benefit provided through Christ's Atonement and was not to be withheld from those who desired its blessing.

Although some healing "campaigners" did arise, The Christian and Missionary Alliance was not to become a healing movement. Simpson made it clear that divine healing was not an end in itself and should be proclaimed as only a part of the full gospel.

The Christian and Missionary Alliance was not designed

to be a church organization. A notable effort was made in the 1912 Council to structure the Alliance as a society that would serve the purpose for which it had been raised. A new constitution was adopted, designating finance, home, foreign, deputation, publication, and education departments, and the local branches were zoned into districts. Local branch superintendents or pastors were to be appointed by the district superintendent "in conjunction with the local committee elected by the branch members." General Council was to be composed of representatives of the branches, giving them more voice in the policies of the headquarters' office.

The new organization was designed to give greater freedom in the cooperation of branches and churches. It was a move that brought increase to the Society, with an awareness of maturity as a united body. The effort to keep independent churches from becoming Alliance churches and to insure that branches were only auxiliaries to established churches began to weaken.

The message and identity of The Christian and Missionary Alliance

Although pressures threatened to eliminate the original design of the Alliance, its identity was marked by a clear, simple focus that was positive in its effect and dynamic in its working. The focus was on the all-sufficiency of Jesus Christ for every believer and the potential of the Spirit-filled life for carrying out the worldwide missionary responsibility. It was Simpson's stated position that the biblical message of the centrality of Christ was being found relevant in all situations as the gospel was taken to neglected places where it had not yet been preached. He believed that revival of neglected truths would involve Christians in the realization of the Alliance "design" based on the great need for world evangelization.

Whether or not others recognized it, The Christian and Missionary Alliance had accepted this role as its calling.

Wherever they met, The Christian and Missionary Alliance adherents came together under a simple and direct statement of the Christian message: "Christ our Savior,

Sanctifier, Healer, and Coming King."

The truth of the Saviorhood of Christ was common within all evangelical groups, but the Alliance vision included the sum total of all that God does for the believer from the time of his new birth to the moment of his final glorification in heaven. The objective as expressed by the founder was to form "a simple and fraternal union of all who hold in common the fullness of Jesus in His present grace and coming glory."

The truth of "Christ our Sanctifier" carried believers a step farther than most denominational teaching of the day. The Spirit-filled life was taught in many groups, but to Simpson and the Alliance people the presence of the Spirit in the life made Christ a bright, daily reality. Holiness was Christ living within, a Person who could meet every human need. Two of Simpson's hymns, "Himself," and "Christ in Me," express his views and experience, emphasizing "Everything in Jesus, and Jesus everything."

It was Simpson's message that Jesus abiding in the believer's heart and life brings into reality all the deeper experiences and truth recorded in the Acts of the Apostles and the New Testament Epistles.

In his view, the believer's throne-right of victory over sin and self and the ministry of the Holy Spirit were to be realized by every believer during his earthly sojourn.

In its essence, Christianity is Christ: to know the fullness of the Holy Spirit is to know the fullness and sufficiency of Christ.

The message of "Christ our Healer" also was to be understood in relation to this context of the adequacy of Christ. The humiliation, corruption, dishonor, and weakness of our mortal bodies spell out an appointment with death until the resurrection, but Christ's provision, ministered through His Spirit, is a quickening of the mortal body in order to fulfill God's redemptive purpose. To live in God's will and in full consecration is to be protected by the omnipotence of Christ.

The proclamation of "Christ our Coming King" held a crowning motivation and represented the hope of the whole world. Satan has usurped authority over creation by subjecting God's creation to the bondage of sin through man's

Fall. Christ has come to proclaim a kingdom that begins with His reign in the hearts of men, then in its ultimate outworking His kingdom will be manifested in restoration and transformation of all creation at Christ's personal return.

This anticipation is associated closely with obedience to Christ's commission: *And this gospel of the kingdom will be preached in the whole world as a testimony to all nations, and then the end will come* (Matt. 24:14). Christ's own presence and authority were promised in the Great Commission: *Therefore go and make disciples of all nations, baptizing them in the name of the Father and of the Son and of the Holy Spirit, and teaching them to obey everything I have commanded you. And surely I will be with you always, to the very end of the age* (Matt. 28:19-20).

Regardless of the weaknesses that contributed to the problem of identity, this Christ-centered message gave substance to the nature and character of the movement. Tozer once said, "What we believe is not as important as what we believe emphatically." The emphatic and positive message undoubtedly saved the Alliance from divisiveness and narrow provincialism.

The nature and character of The Christian and Missionary Alliance in its comprehensive ministry were identified positively by the founder. Simpson and those who worked closely with him felt they owed a public declaration to other evangelical churches and to all associated with their ministry. Probably the fullest and clearest description of The Christian and Missionary Alliance as the founder and president saw it was given at the seventeenth General Council in 1914:

God has given us a missionary movement unique in its polity, worldwide in its scope, lofty in its aims, and inspiring in its motives; and it seems fitting that at this time we should be fully baptized into the very heart of this movement until we ourselves shall go forth as living epistles and apostles for the evangelization of the world.

First and best, it is an evangelical movement, and in these days of doubt and sometimes denial of the Bible and the blood it has ever stood for the faith once for all delivered unto the saints, and steadfastly believed that if we cannot give the world a divine message, we had better give it no message at all.

Second, it is an evangelistic movement, not aiming to build up elaborate institutions, but to preach the Gospel immediately to every creature and give one chance for eternal life to every member of our fallen race.

Third, it is a spiritual movement seeking and sending only missionaries who have been baptized with the Holy Ghost and are fitted to develop the highest type of Christian life among the people to whom they minister.

Fourth, it is an interdenominational movement, not building up sectarianism, but bearing only on its banner the name of Jesus and welcoming the cooperation of Christians and missionaries of every evangelical denomination without requiring the sacrifice of their convictions and denominational relationships.

Fifth, it is an international movement, attracting by the greatness of its scope and interesting by the magnificence of its field men and women who are interested in the welfare of every race and tongue.

Sixth, it is a pioneer movement, not duplicating existing agencies but reaching out to the regions beyond and seeking to send the Gospel to the most destitute corners of this benighted world. In China it was the first to enter the province of Hunan and the pioneer of Kwangsi; in Palestine it built the first American chapel in Jerusalem; in Annam it has planted the first native church; in Venezuela and Ecuador it has dedicated the first Protestant chapels; beyond the Great Wall of China it has thirty-three martyr graves; and the tomb of one of its pioneers is a milestone marking the lonely way to the borders of Arabia.

Seventh, it is an economical movement avoiding expensive establishments, aiming to make every dollar go as far as possible, and sending only such missionaries as are glad to give their lives and services for their bare expenses.

Eighth, it is a premillennial movement, not attempting to convert the world, but rather to gather out of the nations a people for His name and stand looking for and hasting forward the coming of the Lord.

Ninth, it is a lay movement, utilizing agencies for which otherwise the doors had perhaps been closed, and encouraging the consecrated layman, the earnest businessman, the humble farmer boy, the Spirit-filled maiden whom the Master has called to follow in the footsteps of the lowly fisherman of Galilee and create a new battalion in the army of the Lord, the volunteers and irregulars of whom we have no cause to be a-shamed, and who but for this movement might never accomplish their glorious work.

Tenth, its divinest seal is the spirit of sacrifice. While we do not claim a monopoly of self-denial, yet we thank God with deepest gratitude and humility for the men and women in the homeland whose noble gifts for missions are not unworthy to have a place with Mary's anointing and the widow's mite.

With these characteristics, the Alliance was recognized as a predominantly missionary movement. The problem of identification was not by any means solved, but progress had been made and loyalty and faithfulness to the world task remained at high level.

Irregularism: Permanent or Temporary? (1920-1939)

Simpson's reference to "volunteers and irregulars" in point nine of his description of the ministry as a lay movement constituted a unique confession. His bold, courageous leadership had attracted some of the finest, noblest colaborers in the evangelical world, but they were supplementing the evangelical church and seeking to challenge its life and scope of mission through its lay ministry.

In another of his messages Simpson declared:

The missionary interest is the chief business of every Christian. Hitherto the church has struggled for a bare existence and nearly all her energies have been expended in maintaining herself. Henceforth, let us unite in recognizing that the one business of the church's existence is to evangelize the world, that the work of foreign missions is the one business of every minister, every congregation, every Christian; that the call to preach the gospel to every creature is given to every disciple, and that we have no excuse to remain at home unless we can advance the cause of missions better by so doing than if we went abroad.

Preserving the permanent

Within the Alliance, it was not easy to bring about a realization that a lay movement of "irregulars" was not necessarily permanent. Following the passing of the founder, the new leaders felt the need to establish credibility.

The Christian and Missionary Alliance role was affected by leadership change. As Dr. Simpson and others among his original associates began to pass from the scene, the Alliance role of confronting and challenging the churches through their lay people also began to change drastically, even though there was still no anticipation that the lay movement would become a church.

In 1916, the Council reported that there were 300 "localities" and 270 "pastors and evangelists"—implying that the term *branches* was in transition and that the "superintendents" had taken on a new role. The changes reported, however, were subtle and unsupported by the original leaders.

Shortly before the death of Simpson in 1919, a personal incident took place which was later recounted by the incumbent president, Paul Rader:

Dr. Simpson was occupying a room at headquarters across the hall from the Board meeting which he was unable to attend. At the close of the meeting I went into his room with Brother Senft and Brother Lewis. He put out his arm, and we knelt to pray. Oh, such a prayer! He started in thanksgiving for the early days and swept the past in waves of praise at each step, then to the present, then on to the future—the prophetic vision was marvelous. We all, with upturned, tear-stained faces, were praising God together with him as by faith we followed him to the mountain and viewed the Promised

Land. He was so sure the Alliance was born in the heart of God. He lay there in a burst of praise, sure that God could carry it forward. So, reverently he lifted his hands as if passing the work over to God who had carried it all these days.

The new leadership, faced with establishing credibility for Alliance ministers and directors, sought to enshrine the nostalgia of the past. Certainly the establishment of a self-extending, self-governing church, consolidated for the possession of "the Promised Land," was not in their minds at that point.

The Alliance as a movement often was confused with other groups. The Pentecostal movement took for its own use many of the expressions which Simpson had originated. The term *Fourfold Gospel* was often confused with the Four-Square church which began to emerge on the West Coast in the early 1920s. The term "Jesus Only" used by Simpson was also taken to identify a "Jesus Only" Pentecostal sect that denied the personhood of the Father and of the Holy Spirit. The identification of "Full Gospel Tabernacle" was used also by some Pentecostal groups.

A severe rift between the holiness and Pentecostal movements served only to increase the identity problem for those interdenominational movements desiring to be conciliatory and remain in full cooperation with existing evangelical churches.

Perceiving the temporary

While the societal characteristics of the Alliance continued, resistance to becoming a denominational church began to fade. It was sensed, however, that drastic sudden changes could alienate much that was good and essential to the molding and shaping by divine providence.

The Christian and Missionary Alliance interdenominational emphases and structure had a temporary usefulness. With the launching of new movements and sects around them, many existing churches became wary and protective. The support given the Alliance missionary program by established churches had reached its peak even before the death of Simpson. The formation of Alliance branches, openly promoted as disassociated from New Testament church organization, was viewed as an impractical structure by the general public. Because the climate for interdenominational movements had drastically changed, the Alliance would become more and more restricted unless it took on regular ministries of a church.

A survey committee in 1923 reported a total of 153 Alliance branches and 806 *Alliance Weekly* subscribers, but the figures did not rightly reflect the true nature of the Alliance. In 1924, another attempt was made to analyze the strengths and form of the movement. The new report indicated 323 missionary conventions, 325 full-time workers, and 33 new branches. No attempt was made to report membership, *Alliance Weekly* subscribers, or even the total number of organized branches.

From 1924 to 1928, Council reports reflected tensions and debates concerning the possibilities of The Christian and Missionary Alliance becoming sectarian, losing fraternal relations, and putting more stress on church membership.

The report in 1926, revealing a total of 248 church buildings and 96 parsonages owned by Alliance congregations, brought evident consternation to Council. The report also indicated that there were then 365 regularly organized Sunday schools, in spite of the earlier pattern that the Society should not attempt to conduct Sunday schools.

No statistics were made available in the 1928 Council, but the delegates directed a reorganization of the Home Department.

Obviously, The Christian and Missionary Alliance was seeking to establish its identity and form in order to express its worship and to expedite its worldwide mandate. It was being delayed, however, by the inhibitions regarding church identity which it was not yet ready to confront.

The Christian and Missionary Alliance's training of "irregulars" in Bible institutes became impractical for the need of the day. Simpson's early interest in missions had led him to study the training operation of the East London Institute for Home and Foreign Missions, a project founded by H. Graaton Guinness. As a teenage youth, Simpson had heard Guinness speak in his home church in Chatham, Ontario.

The East London Institute served to increase the number of available missionaries, giving particular training to many who lacked proper educational background and means of support for university or seminary studies. In sixteen years, five hundred young men from this school had become workers at home and overseas.

Simpson was led, then, to launch the first Bible institute in America in 1882. It was the New York Missionary Training Institute (now Nyack College). A similar school, Moody Bible Institute in Chicago, began in 1886. Whereas Simpson called his students "irregulars," Moody called his "gap-men." Simpson described the kind of training and preparation he envisioned:

> Early in the history of the Church we find God sending forth laymen like Stephen, Philip and Barnabas to lead the great work of apostolic evangelization. We do not compete in this Institute with the regular theological seminary and the ordinary methods of taking the gospel ministry. We claim to be raising up a band of irregular soldiers for the vast unoccupied fields to supplement the armies of the Lord in the regions they cannot reach and work they cannot overtake (*After Fifty Years*, p. 92).

In 1916, another Alliance Bible institute was begun in the Midwest (now St. Paul Bible College) and in 1921, on the Pacific Coast (now Simpson College). The Bible school movement in North America grew so rapidly that more than two hundred were established within a few decades.

In 1929, The Christian and Missionary Alliance closed a number of smaller schools under its auspices because they were no longer economically practical. Times had changed. The educational tide was rising and the operational style of Alliance training and education had to change with it.

The fact that irregularism was a temporary phase can be observed in the constitutional changes made at Council. The 1935 Council reported 418 "branches and churches." No effort was made to explain the distinction or to give a reason for the change in categories. In 1936, the official manual still carried a constitution for branches which designated a local superintendent instead of a pastor and which had no section on ordinances. But the manual also carried a "Suggested Constitution for Churches" with sections on the duties of the pastor, the elders, and executive board members. Here the ordinances were listed. The obvious changes were muted by the implication that churches were not in reality Alliance churches, since their constitution was only "suggested."

There is no record of the number of Alliance branches that changed their constitutions to become constituted as churches. Many constructed new buildings, and names often were changed from "tabernacle" to "church" without even acknowledging the difference. Yet, overall, The Christian and Missionary Alliance tenaciously continued to call itself a "Society."

Introducing a chapter on the origin and history of the Alliance in *After Fifty Years* in 1939, the president, H. M. Shuman, wrote:

The Christian and Missionary Alliance was raised up by the Lord to fulfill its own peculiar mission and has its place along with other spiritual irregulars. It was not begun because of a division or dissatisfaction among individuals or groups. Rather, it was the natural outcome of the mighty anointing of the Holy Ghost and the heart passion for the lost that possessed its founder, Dr. Simpson, and his associates (p. 16).

"Irregularism" thus had become a designation of status quo rather than a description of the type of ministry the Society was currently fulfilling. Though irregularism had been used originally to promote evangelism and missions among the churches, now it became an identification that related to a past reason for existence.

A Church: to Be or Not to Be? (1940-1974)

The Christian and Missionary Alliance continued to be an interdenominational society in name, if not in fact. The strategy of irregularism was no longer functional and the missionary calling to which it was committed could be fulfilled only through the church as the proper biblical base.

Only as it acknowledged and owned its identification as a church and began multiplying churches could the missionary mandate be carried forward properly. By the time of the beginning of World War II, a notable change was taking place.

A church: indigenous in nature

To reproduce naturally "after its own kind" is the nature of the church for which the term *indigenous* is used. In the beginning the large Alliance missionary conventions had given rise to branches. The former providence had thought it best to utilize neglected forces known as "irregulars" from established churches to carry out the missionary mandate.

The newer, emerging providence was seen in circumstances in which new churches would be formed by discipling new converts and baptizing and teaching them all things that Jesus had commanded. These would form new bases from which missionaries would come and their support would be given.

The Christian and Missionary Alliance in its process of change and growth had become an indigenous church. During the later 1930s and then more particularly between 1940 and 1945, extension of the home base became a predominant theme. Any idea that this was "church planting" and uniquely different from organizing Alliance branches went unrecognized.

The Council in 1940, without distinction of number, reported 546 branches and churches, whereas in 1946 no branches were reported and church membership was said to be 50,146.

Then in 1947, the Home Secretary made this comment in his report to Council:

Bringing up to date the list of certified and operating churches and branches in certain districts has reduced the total number of churches considerably. However, the figure of 939 branches and churches represents greater accuracy and does not include affiliated churches.

Totals of 43,373 members and 7,174 adherents were also reported in 1947.

Obviously, the secretary was attempting to wrestle with

the distinction between churches and branches. That which certified the operation of one or the other was crucial for the accounting, but carried no explanation. The total number of branches and churches had increased from 546 to 939 in seven years, a 72 percent increase which was dramatic in terms of the total past record. A new concept of apostolic church planting was coming into being and the former strategy of "irregularism" was being disowned.

The Christian and Missionary Alliance in its overseas church-planting policy was recognizing the indigenous church. The early Evangelical Missionary Alliance as constituted in 1887 had described its purpose in this way: "It will leave each church established on the foreign field free to organize and administer its affairs as it may choose." The implementation of that stated policy through the years, however, had proven to be difficult.

The Christian and Missionary Alliance planted the first churches in the provinces of Hunan and Kwangsi, China, and constructed the first "American" church building in Jerusalem, the first gospel churches in Viet Nam and Cambodia, and the first Protestant chapels in Venezuela and Ecuador. By 1912, there were 270 missionaries and more than 4,000 self-supporting churches and groups overseas. But to perpetuate them as indigenous churches became more difficult and complex as missionaries sent by the branches tried to transmit overseas that which was not being produced at home. Not only Alliance missionaries but those from independent faith missionary boards as well, realized that self-support was often more important than development of a doctrine of indigenous self-government and self-propagation.

Delegates to the 1927 Council had made a concerted effort to deal with the problem. The following resolution was adopted:

> Resolved, that in order to most effectively promote the growth and development of the native church in each field, we recognize that it may often be wise policy to urge self-government before the church becomes fully self-supporting in those fields where old methods of support through foreign funds have been in effect for

years; but that in the new fields the definite policy of full self-support in the native church should be adhered to.

This policy became most effective in Viet Nam and in Belgian Congo (Zaire), but seemingly made little progress in other countries. Based on the progress of church extension at home, 250 new missionaries were sent overseas between 1945 and 1949, bringing the total to 590 missionaries. Still, for the church at home to produce its counterpart overseas was not easily accomplished where previous policies had become firmly entrenched.

In 1955, the Foreign Department adopted a stringent policy that each overseas church become self-supporting from its inception and that a national church training effort and a viable missionary withdrawal procedure be observed as expeditiously as possible. This was official indication that the way to become an indigenous church was to be the visible church in action, learning to be responsible for its own evangelistic and missionary outreach, as well as sustaining its own worship and nurture ministry. In 1971, the Foreign Secretary drew this line clearly in his statement:

The New Testament sets the church in this world for the purpose of carrying the gospel to the ends of the earth. Altogether apart from financial aid from others, all believers are commissioned to participate in carrying the gospel unto all the world.

A church: practical in operation

The necessity for readjustment to a church identity continued to be felt, although no direct change was recognized regarding The Christian and Missionary Alliance as an interdenominational society. However, as the home church became indigenous in action, various aspects of church life came into focus for necessary change.

The church must identify and declare its doctrine more specifically. In 1960, the president, Harry L. Turner, made this revealing comment to Council:

Rightly or wrongly, the days are past when we were only a fellowship. Today we are a church. We must tell the world what we believe and why we believe it. We are

141

not ashamed of our badge. We want our colleges, our pastors, our missionaries and members to courageously and intelligently say, "This is it." Then and only then will our tomorrow be strong in its God-intended foundation.

As a society, The Christian and Missionary Alliance had maintained a simple statement on membership:

Qualification for membership shall consist of satisfactory evidence of regeneration and belief in God the Father, Son, and Holy Spirit; in the verbal inspiration of the Holy Scriptures as originally given; in the vicarious atonement of the Lord Jesus Christ; in the eternal salvation of all who believe in Him and the eternal punishment of all who reject Him; recognition of the truths of the Lord Jesus Christ as Saviour, Sanctifier, Healer and Coming King, as taught by The Christian and Missionary Alliance; full sympathy with the Society's principles and objects, and cooperation by contributing to its work.

This statement was used consistently on membership cards; but along with the practice of ordaining pastors and missionaries for the regular ministry, the need arose for a more adequate general statement to safeguard the church from error and establish guidelines for leadership training. The following was adopted by Council in 1965.

STATEMENT OF FAITH

1.   There is one God, who is infinitely perfect, existing eternally in three persons: Father, Son, and Holy Spirit.

2.   Jesus Christ is true God and true man. He was conceived by the Holy Spirit and born of the Virgin Mary. He died upon the cross, the Just for the unjust, as a substitutionary sacrifice, and all who believe in Him are justified on the ground of His shed blood. He arose from the dead according to the Scriptures. He is now at the right hand of the Majesty on high as our great High Priest. He will come again to establish His kingdom of righteousness and peace.

142

3.   The Holy Spirit is a divine person, sent to indwell, guide, teach, empower the believer, and convince the world of sin, of righteousness and of judgment.

4.   The Old and New Testaments, inerrant as originally given, were verbally inspired by God and are a complete revelation of His will for the salvation of men. They constitute the divine and only rule of Christian faith and practice.

5.   Man was originally created in the image and likeness of God; he fell through disobedience, incurring thereby both physical and spiritual death. All men are born with a sinful nature, are separated from the life of God, and can be saved only through the atoning work of the Lord Jesus Christ. The portion of the impenitent and unbelieving is existence forever in conscious torment; and that of the believer, in everlasting joy and bliss.

6.   Salvation has been provided through Jesus Christ for all men; and those who repent and believe in Him are born again of the Holy Spirit, receive the gift of eternal life, and become the children of God.

7.   It is the will of God that each believer should be filled with the Holy Spirit and be sanctified wholly, being separated from sin and the world and fully dedicated to the will of God, thereby receiving power for holy living and effective service. This is both a crisis and a progressive experience wrought in the life of the believer subsequent to conversion.

8.   Provision is made in the redemptive work of the Lord Jesus Christ for the healing of the mortal body. Prayer for the sick and anointing with oil are taught in the Scriptures and are privileges for the church in this present age.

9.   The Church consists of all those who believe on the

Lord Jesus Christ, are redeemed through His blood, and are born again of the Holy Spirit. Christ is the Head of the Body, the Church, which has been commissioned by Him to go into all the world as a witness, preaching the gospel to all nations.

The local church is a body of believers in Christ who are joined together for the worship of God, for edification through the Word of God, for prayer, fellowship, the proclamation of the gospel, and observance of the ordinances of baptism and the Lord's Supper.

10. There shall be a bodily resurrection of the just and of the unjust; for the former, a resurrection unto life; for the latter, a resurrection unto judgment.

11. The second coming of the Lord Jesus Christ is imminent and will be personal, visible, and premillennial. This is the believer's blessed hope and is a vital truth which is an incentive to holy living and faithful service.

The church must be evangelistic, propagating its faith in the community as a base of "the pillar and foundation of the truth." Evangelism is to be planned, promoted, and conserved by the church through responsible membership. Baptisms in the Alliance churches at home were first reported as statistics in 1958, even though baptized membership statistics overseas had been included in the Foreign Secretary's reports to Council almost from the beginning. In 1968, evangelism strategies were prepared and promoted from the Home Secretary's office, and churches began to take on new life as self-extending efforts in church growth and a responsible church membership began to be seen as part of its biblical mandate.

Carrying on this kind of evangelism seemed irregular for a society of "branches." Formerly, converts were to be sent to established churches to be baptized and conserved. Although this was no longer practiced, the tradition had not been superseded by any clear mandate. With this inhibition receding, however, evangelism as part of church life was becoming natural and necessary.

The church must be responsible in training leaders for a regular ministry adequate to the needs of the churches. From the training of irregulars in Bible institutes to mobilizing lay leadership for neglected fields, a transition had to be brought about whereby churches could be led by those prepared adequately to preach and to minister. At stake was true development of the spiritual life of the church and full utilization of the gifts the Lord of the church had bestowed upon the members.

Failure to properly identify the branches as churches caused the Bible schools to lean more and more toward serving young people as a ministry in itself rather than training adequate leaders for aggressive evangelism and church development. Failure to train the regular ministry also constituted a loss for the entire Society. In the opinion of many, the close motivational relationship between the spiritual leadership of The Christian and Missionary Alliance and the educational program of the training institute in the beginning days was notably diminished in the forties and fifties in the Bible colleges.

Instead of representing the cutting edge for future leadership development, the Bible colleges in the sixties largely became recruiting centers for terminal ministerial training in various evangelical seminaries, even though ministerial training continued to be offered on the undergraduate level. General studies programs were increased so that some schools became fully accredited as liberal arts colleges.

In 1960, Jaffray School of Missions offered only one year of graduate training for missionaries, but by 1974, it had become the Alliance School of Theology and Missions (now Alliance Theological Seminary) to serve the United States constituency. In 1970, Canadian Theological Seminary was established in Canada for ministerial training.

The church is to be organized in a unified, systematic, and functional manner. Between 1971 and 1974, the Alliance studied and brought about a complete plan of structural reorganization. New relationships were established at the headquarters to provide better coordination and integration of the various ministries, especially to provide a realistic balance between responsibilities of the churches at home and the responsibilities of missionary operations overseas.

The organization of local churches was designed to reflect the involvement of the laity so as to maximize indigenous self-responsibility, improving churchmanship in corporate maturity.

Although "branches" had not been recognized for more than twenty-five years and The Christian and Missionary Alliance no longer was a "society" of people whose membership in a parachurch organization identified the strategy of its operation, the recognition of being a denomination of churches was observed by the president after the final approval of reorganization during General Council. The angularity of this recognition was reflected in a news item in *Eternity* (August 1974) magazine with the heading, "C&M Alliance Converts to Denominational Status." It read:

> After 87 years as a para-denominational organization dedicated to missionary activity, The Christian and Missionary Alliance has officially recognized what many people have known for years: the Alliance is a denomination. By a vote of 834 to 98, delegates to the Alliance's General Council meeting in Atlanta (Georgia) adopted a new constitution and by-laws making the Alliance a denomination.

10

The Christian and Missionary Alliance As a Denominational Church

The credibility of a church body will stand or fall in direct relation to its truthfulness with God's Word and its identification with the universal church of Jesus Christ. About thirteen hundred "families" of churches are said to be representing Christianity in the world today, and it is certain that most of them often are accused of being sectarian.

In its beginning, The Christian and Missionary Alliance identified itself as an "interdenominational society" and recognized denominational structures as biblically valid, rather than being sectarian. Dr. Simpson's early and strong sense of responsibility to the church is revealed in these words:

It is a very solemn thing to be responsible for schism or separation in the church. When we do we sin against the heart of Jesus, we sin against the Holy Ghost, we sin against the very body of Christ.

In an editorial Simpson further warned:

The Christian Alliance is not a sect. It has larger business on hand than breaking down the churches and building up a little denomination. Some of us know the evils that have been caused by the efforts of well-meaning brethren and sisters to break down the existing organizations and gather little companies out of their present fellowship. It is not our object. Let none of our people be misled into it.

The Alliance has never sought advantages that would come at the expense of other churches or denominations. The Alliance has endeavored sincerely to minister as a sacrificial servant of Jesus Christ, for interdependence of churches is vital to their testimony and spiritual effectiveness. George W. Peters makes this observation:

No one can study the symbolic presentation of the church without being deeply impressed by the truth of interdependence. While the Bible upholds the autonomy of the local assembly, it knows nothing of independence in the absolute sense of the word. Biblical independence is always balanced by absolute dependence upon the Lord and interdependence among the churches. Thus denominationalism is not contrary to the Bible. Denominationalism in the sense of larger fellowships, closer cooperation and mutual exchange, and assistance of churches is fully within the framework of biblical teaching and is clearly implied in the symbolic presentation of the church (*A Biblical Theology of Missions*, p. 202).

Principles and Objectives

In Simpson's view, the visible, organized church was necessary, and essential to its spiritual dimension was the believer's personal relationship to Jesus Christ. He taught that nothing would bring a stronger spirit of unity to the church than the anointing of the Holy Spirit to live the Christ life in keeping with God's Word.

The proportion and scope of vision in relation to the need of his day strongly conditioned Simpson's view of the church. His sympathy with the Student Volunteer movement as spearheaded by John Mott was genuine, but he did see the responsibility for the immediate evangelization of the world resting primarily with the whole church of Jesus Christ. Envisioning evangelism and missions as spearheaded by Spirit-filled "irregulars" in denominational churches, Simpson sought to marshal all his energies for that specific purpose.

148

The Christian and Missionary Alliance as a paradenominational society sought earnestly to fulfill Simpson's vision for approximately eighty-five years. However, with changing situations and continuing growth, its own family of churches now seeks to represent Christ by faithful message and by the example of its own function.

A resolution adopted by the 1978 Council to double the constituency by 1987, the centennial year, marked a new consciousness of the challenge to "be" the church and to utilize its full potential to fulfill the Great Commission. To give purpose and direction to every area of its work, the Board of Managers adopted principles undergirded by specific goals and objectives.

Principles of belief for operation

The principles of belief provide a foundation upon which advance is expected and describe the nature of its operation:

- We believe that the glory of God and the highest good of Alliance churches are best served by a structure in which there is a place for local churches, districts, and Headquarters to cooperate at every stage. We believe that a cooperative effort at all levels provides the greatest assurance of spiritual freedom and success.
- We believe there is true ingenuity in each church and district to devise the best, the most economical, the most efficient way to achieve the goals.
- We believe that the Headquarters' responsibility is to make sure that the people's desire as expressed in Council action is properly understood—that the necessary options are thoroughly evaluated before a plan is promulgated.
- We believe that Headquarters' role is to set the criteria, give suggestions, and help provide resources in personnel and finances to assist churches and districts to achieve the goals.

These principles have significant value in any effort to reach a present understanding of The Christian and Missionary Alliance. The identity, dignity, and calling of the local church become the focal point of God's redemptive program. The local church should not be set over against the district office or the national headquarters. The local church must own its primary responsibility in the salvation of souls, the upbuilding of believers, and the recruitment of missionaries. Through preaching the Word, mutual exercise of faith, and voluntarism of service and sacrifice, the local church advances the work of the kingdom.

The district offices and national headquarters are not separate entities, but perform those ministries and functions that the local church cannot perform adequately for itself. They serve as checks and balances in the total operation. Though these offices may appear pyramidal in structure, they are not hierarchal in nature. Through mutual agreements from the grass roots, they serve as constituted authorities for the unifying of vision and faith and the strengthening of resources.

The church in its local and extended family expression must discern how to own its identity with purpose in order to strengthen its ministry and to preserve the faith.

In a sermon titled "The New Testament Pattern of Missions," Simpson recognized that the church of Jesus Christ must have a definite pattern:

This house has a divine pattern. Just as the tabernacle of old was to be constructed strictly according to the pattern that was shown to Moses on the Mount, so the Church of Christ has a divine plan, and should be in every particular constructed accordingly. The failure to do this has been the cause of all the apostasies, declensions and mistakes of the past eighteen centuries, and is the reason that the heathen world is still lying in darkness and crying to God against the unfaithfulness of His people.

Goals and objectives for achievement

The goals and objectives set forth in 1978 were designed for short-term achievement. These, nevertheless, give insight into the primary function of The Christian and Missionary Alliance and its total ministry of discipline in church work. For clarity, a *goal* is defined as a state of being toward which one is heading; *objectives,* as steps taken to

150

achieve a goal. The Board of Managers adopted the following:

- To arrive at a renewal of evangelism—aiming to win the lost:

  By leading believers to spiritual maturity and fruit bearing.

  By emphasizing conversion growth as a major activity of all churches through training of pastors and people, regular evangelistic services and other programs that have proved to be good evangelistic methods.

  By having an annual evangelistic crusade or a series of special evangelistic weekend services in local churches.

  By establishing a Chair of Evangelism, or a suitably strong alternative, at Alliance School of Theology and Missions and at Canadian Theological College, and by an increasing emphasis on evangelism training at all Christian and Missionary Alliance colleges.

  By further developing or coordinating existing programs and initiating new programs that will have a direct bearing on the realization of the goals.

- To secure maximum participation of as many members and adherents as possible according to their evident maturity and ability:

  By some engaging in intercessory prayer for the spiritual health of the local church, for the conversion of sinners in its community, and for the success of this God-ordained enterprise worldwide.

  By some opening their homes for, and others teaching, home Bible studies.

  By some distributing Scriptures and tracts.

  By some giving handsomely and sacrificially large sums of money.

  By some endeavoring to start new churches.

  By some engaging in personal evangelism and some discipling new converts.

- To produce a plan whereby our constituency at church and district level will effectively arrive at their goal setting:

By each District Executive Committee making a study amd determining its goals and strategies.

By means of each Church Governing Board making a study and determining its goals and strategies.

By convening a 5-day Leadership Evangelism Conference at Nyack, N.Y., for Headquarters' executive staff, all district superintendents, field directors of specialized ministries, educators, district Christian education directors, and district extension directors.

By convening 53 continent-wide evangelism seminars early in 1979, with a goal of 10,000 pastors and lay people attending.

By continuous evangelism seminars at district and national levels.

By an evangelism training seminar conducted by each local church.

- To provide a strategy to renew failing and stagnant churches:

    By providing education for district and pastoral leadership relating to the unique problems encountered by the declining church.

    By training district personnel as church growth consultants to work with churches in need.

    By formulating church growth concepts that have direct application to small and declining churches.

    By funding redevelopment programs based on a sharing formula if it seems that the infusion of outside funds will help revitalize the church.

- To plant new churches:

    By existing churches starting new churches.

    By training district and local church leaders in principles of church planting.

    By appointing district extension directors to give oversight in church planting.

    By formulating area strategies of expansion.

- To establish the basis of measuring, evaluating, and reporting progress in attaining goals:

    By quarterly reporting from the churches to district offices and to Headquarters.

    By Headquarters reporting to the entire constituency

quarterly or more often through every available medium: *The Alliance Witness, The Growing Harvest,* all district publications, and Dial-Alliance Missions.

- To infuse interest in Alliance missions in every church:
  By teaching the Bible basis of missions.
  By acquainting the members with our missionary mandate through missionary conventions, mini-missionary conferences, and special missionary retreats.
  By increasing the number of available missionaries by whatever method deemed necessary in order to serve the increased number of churches.
  By communicating missions through the use of literature, films, filmstrips, slides, multimedia, and videotape.
  By encouraging Alliance pastors and lay people to visit mission fields as possible.

- To provide the needed resources to make this advance happen in North America:
  By planning budgets in relationship to the stated goals.
  By concentrating on those efforts that have a direct bearing on the realization of the goals.
  By obtaining both paid and voluntary personnel needed to articulate and to give aid in achieving the goals.

- To provide the needed framework to make this advance happen in the overseas work:
  By requesting all Alliance fields to endeavor to arrive at carefully studied goals through negotiated agreements with the national churches.
  By making the achievement of the goal to double our constituency over the next eight years the major focus of the Division of Overseas Ministries.
  By arranging for each regional director to study church-growth principles.
  By organizing on a regular basis field or regional conferences on church growth for missionaries and na-

tional leaders.

By giving key national leaders training in church growth in North America.

By arriving at imaginative means of obtaining the larger level of financing required.

These goals become specific and practical by the following actions of the Board of Managers:

The dates for measuring the goals set by General Council were established as of April 1, 1979, through March 3, 1987.

Inclusive members for North America were to be calculated as of December 31, 1977—192,000; for overseas as of December 31, 1976—952,000.

A net gain of 840 churches in North America and 5,000 overseas.

A goal of 1,200 active missionaries and 3,200 official workers in North America.

One-third of the five-million-dollar goal set by the 1978 General Council—$1,692,000—was to be added to the annual budget each year for three years as a "global advance fund," distinct from the general operating budget.

When The Christian and Missionary Alliance was reorganized in 1912, Simpson, noting that Colossians 4:12 had a peculiar fitness for the time: *that ye may stand perfectly adjusted in all the will of God,* made these observations:

First, we need to be perfectly adjusted in our loyalty to Christ and at the same time our responsibility to the special trust which He has committed into our hands. There is a so-called loyalty to God which makes one impractical, narrow, and wholly unfitted for loyal service in any human fellowship or any common cause. The Apostle Paul gives us the more attractive picture of that perfect consecration of which he says, "They . . . first gave their own selves to the Lord, and unto us by the will of God." God does not want us to be afraid of losing our consecration by being true to The Christian and Missionary Alliance, by knowing how to keep rank and marching loyally under our standard.

In the next place we believe that our constitution and

government are being adjusted to a more perfect harmony of the central authority and executive control on the one hand, and local freedom and independence of the various districts and branches on the other. Like the great federal system of the national government, we believe that the new order will secure great strength and unity in the center of the work, and perfect liberty in every section and department, and that with perfect order and without friction, "fitly framed together," we shall grow up into all the fullness of God's plan for our far-reaching work.

Further, we are learning more perfectly the right adjustment of our home and foreign work, and the interdependence of each upon the other, the home work as the constituency of the foreign, and the foreign as the outlet and complement of the other. There is no cause for jealousy in regard to the support of either. Even our educational work, whose foundations are at present being enlarged, is as essential to the effectiveness of our foreign missions as to the equipment of our home branches. On the other hand, our foreign work is not only the fulfillment of the supreme duty of the Church of Christ, but the loftiest inspiration and uplift of our whole Christian life at home.

Again, we need to be perfectly adjusted to old, conservative traditions and new, progressive ideas, methods and movements. God grant that this work may never lose its old simplicity, self-sacrifice and separation, not only from the secular but from the religious world in its spirit and practice. But at the same time we must keep abreast of the progress of our age and be men and women of today in our message and ministry to our own generation.

Once more, we need to be adjusted on the one hand to our own particular sphere of service and the organized work which God has given us as our peculiar trust, and yet to the larger fellowship of the whole body of Christ. Our new constitution recognizes this larger community in emphatic and timely words. We cannot afford to allow any narrow or sectarian spirit to cut us off from the largest catholicity. We need our brethren of every Christian name, and it is still true, *whether Paul, or Apollos, or Cephas ... all are yours.* The whole Church of Christ needs our message and the inspiration of our spirit and our work, and we need the fellowship and uplift of all saints. Let it therefore be our high ideal and aim and prayer that this blessed work may ever stand perfectly adjusted in all the will of God.

Organization and Administration

A. W. Tozer wrote concerning the true life of the church:
  The throbbing heart of the church is life—in the happy phrase of Henry Scougal, "The life of God in the soul of man." This life, together with the actual presence of Christ within her, constitutes the church a divine thing, a mystery, a miracle. Yet without substance, form and order this divine life would have no dwelling place, and no way to express itself to the community.

Though the church cannot properly exist without official organization and a church order, these must at all times remain as instruments of faith in recognition of Christ's Lordship by His Word and Spirit. The reorganization in the Alliance brought about between 1971 and 1974 provided coordination and integration of the various ministries but, because the church is not a static institution, adjustment to change and progress will continue. Certain basic elements identify The Christian and Missionary Alliance as a denomination of churches.

The local church
  Each local church is more than a subdivision of the denomination: rather, organically and organizationally, it is the church of Jesus Christ. The church is not made by adding together the local churches, nor can it be broken down into them; each is a full manifestation of the church of God.

  The principle of responsible decision making at the most common level is inherent to the nature of the church. Any supralocal dimension of organization and office exists for the local church and is prescribed by the highest legislative assembly by proper representation.

The form of government is a combination of elements of the congregational and presbyterian systems. Local churches are not wholly entities unto themselves but are related externally through the national and district organizations. A constitution of the local church establishes its identity, relationship, membership, ordinances, and basic rules of government. Considerable self-determination is expressed by the local church through its bylaws.

A meeting of the membership is held annually when official and departmental reports are given, business is conducted, and officers are elected. A governing board with a majority of elders or of elders exclusively gives spiritual and administrative oversight to the local church and conducts the affairs of the church between annual meetings. It is amenable to the membership and to the district executive committee through the superintendent.

An Alliance church is a missionary church, constitutionally bound to hold an annual missionary conference. Designated missionary tours are arranged through the district office at which time faith promises are received for the worldwide work. The Division of Overseas Ministries is responsible to the local church to encourage their investment and interest in prayer and through sending missionaries. The church and the mission cooperate where mutual concerns and responsibilities converge.

The district

In the New Testament the word *church* is used to describe groups of believers in their different localities. Both singular and plural forms are used variously. In the book of Acts, and again in the book of Ephesians, the word *church* is used in the supralocal sense. Even though the relationship between the local churches and the whole church is not explored, it is never a disconnected jumble of isolated and self-sufficient fellowships. United through individual service and fellowship, the New Testament church embraces an encompassing fellowship.

The Christian and Missionary Alliance presently has twenty-four districts in the United States and Canada. Additional responsibilities in Hawaii, Mexico, Puerto Rico, Guatemala, and the Dominican Republic, along with ethnic churches, are governed by a special division at headquarters. Each of the larger ethnic groups has its own director and church conference. These "specialized ministries" are represented by nearly three hundred churches.

The districts, under the supervision of superintendents, form a liaison between the national offices and the local churches. Each annual district conference, comprised of representatives from the churches, acts as a legislative body, electing the superintendent and the executive committee and appointing special committees to administer matters such as church extension, ordination of pastors, licensing of workers, and ministries in Christian education, camps, and conventions. Each church may be represented by the pastor and two lay delegates for the first 150 members. In addition, the church may send one delegate for each additional 100 members. All official workers residing in the district also are included as delegates.

The district organization performs those functions for the local church which are suitable on a cooperative basis, especially to supply candidates to churches in need of a pastor, to give guidance where special problems arise, to establish new churches, and to direct special projects. The district superintendent functions as a third party with the pastor and the local church when needed. Each local church carries on its work with a freedom in independence that encourages initiative and responsibility in its own community.

General Council/General Assembly

The highest legislative body of The Christian and Missionary Alliance is the General Council in the United States and the General Assembly in Canada. Ultimate power is vested in the entire membership of the local churches through representation similar to the district conferences. All credentialed workers (including army chaplains, institutional chaplains, and evangelists) are also official delegates. In the United States, Council meets annually, while in Canada the Assembly meets biennially.

The meeting of the Council/Assembly perhaps renders its

highest service in the inspiration it offers as a survey is given by the president and reports are considered from the various departments. It is best described by the word *synergism,* meaning "cooperative action of discrete agencies such that the total effect is greater than the sum of the separate effects taken independently." Particularly is this true of the overseas ministries as reports from the various countries are given, bringing into focus the representative ministries of the churches through missionaries. The climax of Council/Assembly is a festive missionary rally on the last day.

The missionary reports together with the survey of district ministries, specialized ministries, and various projects serve to highlight not only what God has done but also the opportunities and needs that concern the churches in their service to Jesus Christ. Special committees are assigned to study the reports and bring in recommendations for consideration and action.

One of the main responsibilities of the Council/Assembly is the election of the officers and members of the board who give direction to the national offices and departments between meetings. Their responsibility is to use the funds of the denomination wisely and to direct an almost endless agenda of new situations and problems as they arise in the overseas work and the districts.

Lines of communication to the constituency are maintained through *The Alliance Witness, The Canadian Alliance News,* and district periodicals.

The headquarters in the United States and in Canada have an important ministry of coordinating and disseminating the overall work of the denomination. The president, his cabinet, and the Board of Managers or Directors must carry out the will of the General Council or General Assembly. Their service must demonstrate the best interests of the districts and churches and of the missionary conferences and representatives overseas. They must give guidance and supervision to the work of publications, higher education, missionary appointments, and seeking to generate vision and intercessory prayer concerning the overall work of the denomination. The responsive concern of leadership at this level contributes much to every area of the global enterprise.

The Alliance has experienced an unusual and highly profitable spirit of harmony in its overall work. A check-and-balance government achieves effective action that protects local freedom and independence in the various districts and churches.

The Alliance World Fellowship

Founded in 1975, the nonlegislative Alliance World Fellowship gives national church leaders overseas the opportunity to review church growth in the various countries of Alliance ministries. Their vision is to coordinate the national church and missions advance around the world and to witness to the worldwide unity of Alliance believers in the body of Christ.

The Alliance World Fellowship meets every four years. As national church leaders come together to share their victories and concerns, new vision and understanding are cultivated. Emergency needs, such as relief for refugees and the rapid urbanization of the Third World are prayerfully considered for appropriate action. The Alliance World Fellowship, as a united nations for evangelization, is only a foregleam of the day when every tribe, tongue, and nation will be represented around the throne of the Lamb.

Support Services and Auxiliary Enterprises

Soon after Pentecost, the early church had to govern its communal existence and adjust its organization to care for its widows. The demands of our generation call for change but not for irresponsibility or disintegration. As the church confronts new challenges and needs, it must function in new ways to strengthen its ministry while at the same time observing scripturally sound principles, practices, and concepts.

Support services

Support services are those that relate directly to the

ministry of the churches but which individual churches cannot provide adequately for themselves or which are carried on in churches but are notably strengthened and helped with interchurch administration.

Christian education. Churches need help in providing adequate curriculum and materials that will serve the particular needs of the churches and the families in the churches. There are a number of good evangelical publishers that provide excellent materials and who compete commercially, theologically, and philosophically among the denominations, but a particular denomination needs to maintain its own responsibility and initiative in such an important ministry.

The corporate need to guide individuals through definite stages of spiritual development and usefulness that relate to the church's convictions and objectives cannot be relinquished carelessly. The Christian and Missionary Alliance maintains a department of Christian education that seeks to give guidance and direction as well as promotion and inspiration to the churches, and also has some liaison with the Christian education divisions in the colleges and seminaries.

Among the important denominational publications is *The Alliance World,* published quarterly, which provides a curriculum course on missions for various age levels and agencies. Another publication, *The Alliance Teacher,* features articles and helps for the church's Christian education program. The Christian Life and Ministry curriculum for adults is based on the scriptural concept that God has commissioned the church to equip all believers to use their gifts to serve Him. Christians are nurtured to maturity as teaching, training, and service are interrelated in a total church educational program.

The Alliance Witness. While the Canadian Alliance and districts in the United States and Canada and mission headquarters in various countries overseas provide tabloids of news, *The Alliance Witness* is the official organ of the entire constituency, representing its message and mission around the world. It coordinates and projects the self-image of the denomination and serves to tie the Alliance family together in fellowship and service.

Colleges and seminaries. Four undergraduate colleges serve the United States constituency: Nyack College, St. Paul Bible College, Simpson College, and Toccoa Falls College (affiliated). All have Bible and theology departments to prepare young people for Christian service, as well as general studies in preparation for various vocations. The Alliance Theological Seminary and Simpson Graduate School offer graduate training for pastoral and missionary service.

In Canada the Canadian Bible College and Canadian Theological Seminary offer church vocational training on undergraduate and graduate levels respectively.

These schools represent the commitment of the Alliance to leadership in evangelism and missions and a program of education that has grown through a century of experience—from the first Bible institute in North America to a nationwide system of four-year colleges, a one-year graduate school, and two full-fledged three-year seminaries.

As the schools in leadership training go, so go the churches. What Christian education is today, the churches will be tomorrow. Members of The Christian and Missionary Alliance will reach the centennial goals of 95 new missionaries and 150 new pastors a year only as they support intelligently their schools of higher learning.

Organizations of Alliance men and women. Men and ladies of The Christian and Missionary Alliance have strengthened their ministries through becoming organized, not only in the local church, but also on the district and national levels.

For several decades the Alliance Men's organization has grown as a support ministry to provide Christian fellowship among laymen, to encourage Christian witnessing and intercessory prayer, and to assist in extension and missionary interests of The Christian and Missionary Alliance. Hundreds of men have gone overseas to assist in building projects and relief work. A periodical, *Men in Action,* with a circulation of more than twenty thousand, keeps the constituency informed of the ministries of Alliance Men.

The Alliance women's organization had its beginning in

1914 when Mary Rader, Cora Rudy, and Ella Rudy asked other ladies in attendance at General Council in Chicago to come together to pray for missions. In 1929, the Alliance Board of Managers voted to encourage the formation of women's prayer groups. In 1961, the name Women's Missionary Prayer Fellowship was adopted and in 1965, the first national president was elected.

With general coordination by the national organization, every Alliance missionary now is given prayer support and material aid through the interest and ministries of more than twelve hundred local groups. More than a half million dollars is given annually by the women. Included in this is one major missionary project. Specialized ministries are also included in their giving, and some groups have developed evangelistic ministries among women through the local church.

Lay involvement in a global vision has characterized the Alliance and is a needed demonstration of missionary obedience among the millions of Protestants who give less than twenty cents a week for foreign missions. Only through vital and active participation will the church have an impact on a world desperately in need of the gospel.

Auxiliary enterprises

Auxiliary enterprises are those self-supporting corporations that, although relating indirectly to the church, are designed to fulfill vital and necessary services on behalf of The Christian and Missionary Alliance.

Christian Publications, Inc. Publishing has been a significant ministry almost from the beginning of Alliance history. Besides his 1880 publication of *The Gospel in All Lands; The Word, Work and World* in 1882; *The Christian Alliance* in 1888; *The Christian Alliance and Foreign Missionary Weekly* in 1889 (which became *The Alliance Weekly* and later *The Alliance Witness*), Simpson published more than seventy volumes. He wrote 167 hymns and numerous tracts. He established his own publishing house in 1883. From that time the organization has never been without a publication ministry, publishing not only Simpson's books but also those of many others who have contributed to the worldwide ministry of the Alliance.

For more than twenty-five years The Christian and Missionary Alliance produced its own Sunday school materials for all ages in the International Sunday School Lesson series. The adult lesson series is still produced. *Hymns of the Christian Life* was first published in 1891. A second edition was published in 1897 and a third in 1904. These three volumes were combined in 1908. Other editions have since appeared in 1936, 1962, and 1978. Song, with its message and inspiration, is one of the most significant characteristics of the Alliance.

Christian Publications, Inc., Camp Hill, Pennsylvania, is a vital link of communication and corporate body life within the constituency.

Retiral centers. The ministry of caring for the retired, especially missionaries and pastors, has been a growing responsibility. Two centers are managed by The Christian and Missionary Alliance corporately: Shell Point Village in Fort Myers, Florida, and Town and Country Manor in Santa Ana, California. Others are the Alliance Home of DeLand, Florida; the Alliance Home in Carlisle, Pennsylvania; and CAMA Woodlands Nursing Home, Burlington, Ontario, Canada. Altogether, these retiral centers serve more than sixteen hundred residents. Additional retiral centers are being developed by local churches.

This late twentieth-century phenomenon reflects a social responsibility with an unmeasured spiritual ministry.

This outline of The Christian and Missionary Alliance as a denomination is necessarily brief, covering the principal and major aspects of historical development.

Two things remain to be added in summary, and they relate to the unchanging message and objectives of the Alliance, from the beginning to the present day.

Dr. A. B. Simpson, while identifying himself with the evangelical denominational church at large, expressed his vision and desire for the thrust of the Alliance fellowship in 1892:

> Let our churches exist for this; let our ministers preach for this; let our seminaries and colleges be on fire with this one theme; let our laborers toil for this;

let our businessmen carry on their business for this; let our consecrated women sacrifice for this; let our homes be furnished and our wardrobes be purchased with reference to this; and let a whole army of true hearts prove to the whole world around and the heavens above that they understand the meaning of the cross of Calvary, the cry of dying souls, and the glory of the Coming Kingdom.

Then, eighty-eight years later, in his report to the 1980 Council, the president, L. L. King, described the unchanged and continuing purposes of the Alliance with this conclusion:

While in the process of time the society aspect of the Alliance has gradually emerged into a denomination, the particular and special purpose of the organization remains the same. Instead of being a society of believers fellowshipping around a message and a mission, we are now a church with the same message and the same mission. Only the organizational structure has changed. The purpose remains constant.

11

The Christian and Missionary Alliance in Canada

The development of The Christian and Missionary Alliance in the States cannot be traced without acknowledging its roots in Canada. Both the founder, A.B. Simpson, and his closest associate, Henry Wilson, came originally from Canada. Others of Canadian stock who stood tall among the early leaders were R.A. Jaffray, Walter A. Turnbull, E.D. Whiteside, John Salmon, William Fenton, P.W. Philpott, A.W. Roffe, R.H. Glover, David W. LeLacheur, Walter H. Oldfield, and Harry L. Turner.

That the Alliance in Canada coexisted with the Alliance in the United States for almost a century reveals how well a common heritage bound them. When the Alliance in Canada became autonomous in 1981 the church united in the States was almost five times the size of the church in Canada, but the Canadian entity is a unique and natural reflection of its counterpart.

Most of Canada's 25 million people live within two hundred miles of the 49th parallel stretching 4,725 miles from Halifax, Nova Scotia, to Victoria, British Columbia—the world's longest undefended border. From the beginning, pastors could serve in either country and Canadian missionaries could retain their citizenship although sent out by an agency headquartered in New York. Despite many political, social, and economic affinities some inherent factors began to surface as Canadian nationalism and government restrictions developed. Finally, in 1981, the inevitable division came.

The Need for an Indigenous Church

The gospel rightly conceived will root itself in native soil. The citizens who live by that gospel are charged to observe a respectful relationship to the civil government that is designed to protect their rights and privileges (Rom. 13:1-5).

The church as an organism requires a flexible organization that allows it to serve the condition and needs of the people as completely as possible. Therefore, the church must order its housekeeping accordingly, both in the local community and in the nation as a whole. The extension of the local church as a denomination is to enlarge and to strengthen its ministry nationally and in missionary work internationally.

An awakening to this need emerged when the first all-Canadian tridistrict conference was held in 1967 in Regina in observance of Canada's centennial. Fifteen discussion groups formulated articles of declaration on the theme "Guidelines for Tomorrow." In 1969, the president of The Christian and Missionary Alliance called together the representatives of the three districts to discuss a charter for the Alliance in Canada. Then, in 1972, a petition for a federal charter was registered. A second tridistrict conference was held in 1974 in Regina. Officers for a Canadian corporation were appointed, as well as a general director to coordinate and to direct home missions.

In 1975, a study commission was appointed to evaluate the need for Canadian autonomy and to prepare tentative plans for its implementation. The philosophy presented was for a lean, efficient organization that would give proper autonomy to districts and to local churches. It would unite the churches through an interdependence that would minister to the provincial and national needs of Canada as well as to a worldwide missionary responsibility. The overseas missionary ministries would still be carried on in cooperation with the headquarters in New York, for the foreseeable future. However, the missionary funds and personnel would be represented by a personnel and recruitment office in Canada.

This plan, presented in a third conference in 1978, was adopted by a strong 87 percent majority vote. Confident courage emerged as the unanimity of mind and unity of spirit prevailed. Certainly the time had come for Canadians to identify themselves more fully as a national entity and to orient themselves for new and challenging responsibilities.

A formal Canadian church of The Christian and Missionary Alliance became a reality in 1980 when a General Assembly convened at Winnipeg, Manitoba. A provisional constitution was adopted. Officers chosen included Melvin P. Sylvester, president; Gerald L. Fowler, executive vice-president; Arnold P. Reimer, secretary; G. Lloyd Matheson, treasurer; and Arnold L. Cook, director of personnel and missions. This founding assembly, attended by 530 official and 170 corresponding delegates, chose a board of directors and made other necessary appointments. Autonomy became effective on January 1, 1981, thus recognizing a policy of church indigeneity that had been applied for years in the overseas countries, but had been peculiarly neglected in terms of relevance to Canada, where for ninety-five years the Alliance had functioned in effective union with the organization in the United States.

Early beginnings

A number of factors were related to the beginnings of the Alliance in Canada late in the nineteenth century. Among them was a new interest in interdenominational movements which appeared to follow in the wake of recognized spiritual renewal. Certainly, one influence was the Fulton Street revival which began in New York City in 1858.

Another factor plainly was an evident and growing interest in the subject of divine healing, with both secular and religious journalists publishing many stories and accounts of incidents related to "faith cures" and "prayer cures."

While the secular mind was being attracted by the philosophical significance of organic evolution and the growth of experimental sciences, there was dissatisfaction with the status quo in the established churches as modernism and liberalism began to challenge evangelical doctrines.

In the Toronto area, for instance, the Prophetic Conferences on the Niagara attracted international notice. In New York state the Sunday School Union was established in 1874, resulting in large meetings at Chautauqua Lake. The Moody-Sankey meetings found great support both in Britain and in America. The Student Volunteer Movement and other missionary organizations began to challenge the Christian conscience in new and effective ways.

The impact of the divine healing emphasis at that time can be understood, particularly in the light of the concern of evangelical Christian forces about attitudes which indicated strong moves toward a humanistic society.

The divine healing reports, it must be said, were not confined to isolated incidents. Christians, particularly in the circle of evangelical movements, heard intriguing stories of the healing ministries of Dorothea Trudel of Mannendorf, Switzerland; Johannes Blumhardt of Mottlingham, Germany; Elizabeth Baxter and William E. Boardman of London; Charles Cullis, an Episcopalian physician, of Boston; Andrew Murray of South Africa; A. J. Gordon, a Baptist minister, of Boston; R. A. Torrey, president of Moody Bible Institute, of Chicago, and others.

When A. B. Simpson began his ministry in the New York Gospel Tabernacle in 1881, he made little mention of divine healing for his priority was evangelism among the neglected of the city.

On July 2, 1881, President James Garfield was wounded by an assassin's bullet. Simpson told friends in New York that he felt a particular urgency to pray for the recovery of the stricken leader. After the death of Garfield eighty days later, Simpson confessed that an inward voice had prompted him during the interim, "Will you go?"

Some have drawn the conclusion that in response to his sense of neglected duty, Simpson was soon stirred to begin the public divine healing meetings every Friday afternoon in the Tabernacle. Incidents in these services often were reported in the press, in Canada as well as in the States.

Simpson's healing ministry through these reports became

a matter of special interest to a Canadian pastor, John Salmon, of the College Street Baptist Church near Toronto. Salmon had already been struggling with the subjects of sanctification and divine healing and had taken great interest in the ministries of Dorothea Trudel, George Mueller, and William E. Boardman. He determined to visit Mueller in Glasgow, Scotland, his own childhood home, and then to visit Boardman in London.

The meeting of John Salmon and A. B. Simpson

In Glasgow and in London, Salmon became convinced of the importance of the doctrine of divine healing and necessity of sanctification for life and service. Returning to Toronto, he was offered the pulpit of a Baptist church, but chose instead a ministry among sailors and soldiers in the Niagara area, preaching salvation, sanctification, and divine healing.

Being a strong churchman, however, he eventually accepted a call to become the pastor of the Hazelton Avenue Congregational Church in Toronto. He also became involved in the founding of the Toronto Mission Union, promoted by his friend William Howland, with whom he had been associated earlier in the Christian Sailor's Home. Among those serving on the board of the Union was Jonathan Goforth, then a student at Knox College in Hamilton, the seminary where A. B. Simpson received his training.

Even though he was pastor, Salmon realized that he did not have full freedom in his church to emphasize his newly settled doctrinal convictions. He did feel free to contribute to spiritual ministries at the Toronto Mission and with small groups in his own home. In the meantime, Margaret Scott, a Presbyterian, who had become ill at age fifteen with a spinal disease, experienced a miraculous healing. Although she had been paralyzed and in pain for three years and diagnosed as incurable and terminal by physicians, she had made an appointment with Dr. Charles Cullis in Boston in 1882. As a witness of her healing, she began to minister as an evangelist at the age of eighteen and became a personal friend of John Salmon.

Another remarkable healing in Canada was that of Ellen

Hatch. She had been a semiparalytic for seventeen years and leading physicians both in the United States and Canada had not been able to help her. She experienced divine healing under the preaching of Charles Ryder, a Quaker who preached the fourfold gospel and who eventually became an evangelist with the Christian Alliance. Mrs. Hatch was directed by Ryder to John Salmon and she told of her healing in one of his small group meetings. The significance of these healings and others brought divisive reactions to the Hazelton Avenue Congregational Church in Toronto.

Though Salmon had seen remarkable answers to prayer and healings in the group meetings in his home, he himself became afflicted with a kidney disease and, in spite of prayer and heart searching, could not find relief. When the disease began to threaten his personal survival he determined to attend Simpson's "Deeper Life Convention" in Buffalo, New York, in 1885. Despite great pain and difficulty, Salmon made the trip and heard the fourfold gospel under Simpson's preaching. He suddenly felt his own convictions were affirmed. Anointed during an afternoon service, he received deliverance for his physical body and a new vision for his spiritual ministry.

Returning to Toronto, Salmon gave a written account of his healing which occasioned his resignation from the Hazelton church. He then began to preach the fourfold gospel, first holding services in a residence and later in a rented building known as Wolsely Hall.

Meanwhile, a Plymouth Brethren friend of considerable influence, William Fenton, had become afflicted with epilepsy. He, with Salmon, visited Simpson's October convention in New York in 1886 and received healing from the Lord. Subsequently, he became a helpful supporter of Salmon in Toronto, along with William Howland, who by that time had become mayor of Toronto.

Development in the East

When The Christian Alliance and The Missionary Alliance were organized in Old Orchard, Maine, in 1887, both Salmon and Fenton were elected as officers. Salmon remained vice-president for twenty-five consecutive years.

At the earlier Buffalo convention in 1885, a delegation from Hamilton had invited Simpson to Canada. Among them was an official of the Methodist church, R. L. Whyte, and two Presbyterians, a pastor and elder. A committee of five, including Salmon and Fenton, was appointed to plan a convention in Hamilton, where Simpson had begun his ministry.

A founding convention was held in February 1889, at the First Methodist Church in Hamilton. William Howland was elected president and William Fenton secretary. The list of vice-presidents included John Salmon, Margaret Scott, Ellen Hatch, Mr. Hobbs from Ottawa, Mr. Dodds from Kingston, and Dr. Alexander from Montreal. This organization, functioning as a Dominion Auxiliary, represented the Alliance in Canada. A local Hamilton branch was formed with Whyte as president; Mrs. M. Brennen, daughter of Simpson, as vice-president; and Alexander MacKenzie as secretary. A total of 250 cards were signed by those joining the fellowship of the newly formed branch.

Three months later, an Alliance convention was held in Toronto, with thirteen hundred persons attending. A local branch with more than three hundred members was organized, and Salmon was elected president. His Wolsely Hall showed an immediate increase, but Salmon found that his own church orientation could not be set aside quickly and easily.

After two years, however, in 1891, Wolsely Hall became Bethany Chapel, organized as "an undenominational church on Congregational lines," with a membership of ninety, including William Howland. In taking this step, Salmon reasoned that the New York Gospel Tabernacle was "an undenominational church on Congregational lines," so he followed its organizational pattern, naming elders, deacons and deaconesses, and conducting regular observances of the ordinances.

Today, we can only assume that those who composed this early Canadian group faced conflicts and frustrations. They had to try to become adjusted to a Dominion Auxiliary, worship as a branch as well as a church, give loyalty to the presidents of The Christian Alliance organizations and, finally, take direction from the pastor. Along with that situation, Salmon had soon initiated similar Bethany chapels at Hopeville and Peterborough. Since his duties forced him to be away from the Toronto chapel much of the time, he ordained Reuben Zimmerman, a dentist and lay preacher, to serve as associate pastor. The records show that Simpson was a participant in the ordination.

These developments so disturbed William Fenton, basically a Plymouth Brethren, that he withdrew from his position with The Christian Alliance. Another loss was that of William Howland, who died in 1894.

In the meantime, Simpson was proceeding with interdenominational missionary conventions in Methodist, Presbyterian, Congregational, and Baptist churches. Many invitations came from those who were reading reports of the work in his missionary magazine. He conducted more than fifty conventions in Canada: from New Westminster and Vancouver in British Columbia to Winnipeg and Brandon in Manitoba and Ottawa and Montreal in the East. It is plain that his greatest response came throughout the Toronto area. Hundreds of thousands of dollars were raised for missions, and Alliance branches were organized as interest demanded. Missionary candidates were ordained to their ministries at these conventions without any recognition that this actually was a declaration of church planting and establishment.

How Salmon adjusted to Simpson's popularity and methods in Canada is not in the record. However, four of the first fellowships established by Salmon under The Christian Alliance were actually organized as churches along the same lines as the original Wolsely Hall fellowship. It is apparent that these were organized as independent churches in affiliation with The Christian Alliance, while other groups were organized as branches.

The need for training leaders
The inevitable disenchantment among church loyalists gradually set in after the virgin soil in eastern Canada was broken for the Alliance.

173

The method of using branches for Christian Alliance expansion was prevailing, so the interdenominational policy became a matter of trust. Yet, the consolidation of Alliance fellowships became more and more necessary in order to sustain the missionary commitment that now dominated the movement.

In this process of consolidation, hard choices between church and branch became inevitable among those in the branches where double memberships were common. The work in the branches began to shrink rapidly, often because the ordinances were not observed and leaders had no pastoral training.

This pressing need for a training base for Canadian workers caused Salmon to investigate the possibility of a school on the pattern of Simpson's institute at Nyack. As a result, the Toronto Missionary Training Institute was launched in 1893, Salmon tying it in with the ministries at Bethany Chapel.

When the Walmer Baptist Church, however, proposed an interdenominational Bible school in 1894, Salmon felt obliged to cooperate and was present when the school, now known as Ontario Bible College, was organized. This institution, however, did not adequately serve the needs of the Alliance as Salmon had thought it would. When The Christian Alliance and The Missionary Alliance were united to become The Christian and Missionary Alliance in 1897, the Dominion Auxiliary was discontinued and the New York office was designated as the international headquarters. Salmon was appointed first superintendent of the District of Canada, until, in 1899, three districts were formed with one comprising central and northern Ontario, another western and southwestern Ontario, and a third covering eastern Ontario and Quebec. While licensed under provincial charters, the districts were independent of each other, which served to diffuse the Alliance identity in Canada. The very ambiguity with which the Alliance functioned as an organization may be blamed for the slow progress of the Canadian operation in the years that followed.

Blessed and wondrous things continued to happen, nevertheless. Salvation Army Brigadier Peter W. Philpott joined with The Christian and Missionary Alliance, worked closely in its fellowship, and then formed an association of loosely connected independent churches that later became the Associated Gospel Churches of Canada.

Roland Bingham, tutored by Salmon, pastored the Alliance branch near Guelph and then served as assistant pastor at the Bethany Church in Peterborough. Later he joined Walter Gowans of England in promoting and organizing a mission to the African Sudan. Bingham actually founded the Sudan Interior Mission, which now maintains a staff of about twelve hundred missionaries. Salmon was an early council member of this mission. Bingham served as its chairman until retirement.

After the turn of the century, when Salmon had reached the age of sixty-nine, he moved on to live in retirement in California. Early in the 1900s, the three Canadian districts were reduced to one, as the work in eastern Canada tended to blend into that in the eastern section of the United States and many Canadian students chose to attend the Nyack Institute. Some of the pastors and superintendents who served in Canada came from the States and, in turn, many Canadians were pastors of branches in the States, removing much of the Canadian identity.

By the early twenties, the Parkdale Tabernacle Church in Toronto, organized in 1903 by Salmon, suffered severely for lack of pastoral leadership. A young Presbyterian minister, Oswald J. Smith, became the pastor shortly before special meetings were planned in Massey Hall with the Bosworth brothers, renowned for combining evangelism and an emphasis on divine healing. The protracted meetings attracted thousands, resulting in many conversions and testimonies of healing.

While the meetings were still in progress Smith began to plan for the future. He ordered a large tent to be manufactured by the Eaton Company and scheduled further campaigns after the Bosworths had departed. Evangelist Paul Rader, then Alliance president, aided by the Cleveland Colored Quintette, continued to draw large crowds. Based on this kind of interest, Smith initiated the construction of a large Alliance tabernacle seating two thousand people.

Pastor Smith, a dynamic preacher with a gift of keen spiritual vision, revealed a unique sense of church public relations. He edited three papers, one of which, *The Canadian Alliance*, publicized the Alliance work in the Dominion, as well as its international ministry in missions. His vision and concern for western Canada was reflected in a brief paragraph printed in August 1924:

It is conservatively estimated that there are 2,000 organized school districts in our prairie provinces where there are no Sunday schools or Gospel meetings of any kind during the year.

The critical need for trained leadership throughout the Dominion gave birth to the Canadian Bible Institute in 1924, under the able leadership of Dr. Walter Turnbull, former dean of Nyack Missionary Training Institute. The school was located adjacent to the Alliance Tabernacle in Toronto and also accommodated the district headquarters.

Smith had become the district superintendent for eastern Canada, but problems of administration plagued the three operations conducted in such close proximity. After a brief tenure, Smith left the district office to pastor an Alliance branch in California. Within two years, however, he returned to Toronto to launch an independent congregation. Now known as The People's Church, it has become known internationally for the largest annual missionary contributions of any church in North America. Unfortunately, the economic crash in 1929 necessitated closing the Bible institute, but from among its alumni came two imaginative and loyal pioneers for The Christian and Missionary Alliance in western Canada, Gordon Wishart and Willis H. Brooks. For years, their ministries gave direction to Alliance development in the great areas of western Canada.

The double effect of the great economic crash and the loss of many members to The People's Church proved to be a difficult hurdle to overcome. Disjointed from its Canadian heritage and without a training base, owning a history checkered with an ambivalent identity between church and branch, the Alliance in eastern Canada barely survived during the next two decades. In 1929, churches and branches numbered 23; in 1943, only 22. The rebound of eastern

Canada did not come about until after World War II, with the number of churches gradually increasing to 27 by 1950.

Development in the West

Disparity in Canada between its various regions—the Maritimes, French Canada, Ontario, the Prairies, and the Far West—has been exceptionally strong. Even for the churches, the East was East and the West was West and the two knew little of working relationship. The 1300-mile stretch between Toronto and Winnipeg was almost wilderness before the modern highways were constructed.

When Simpson began the New York Gospel Tabernacle in 1881, the population of what is now known as the province of Alberta was approximately 18,000, mainly native Canadians and Metis, fur traders and a few Catholic priests. This population increased to 185,000 in 1906, doubled in five years to 374,000, and then increased by 100,000 immigrants every five years until 1921.

To a large extent, population growth was due to the development of Marquis wheat in 1908, a grain that could mature in a shorter, cooler growing season. Colony settlements and diverse ethnic communities tended to exist largely in isolation. The main binding element and influence was the United Farmers of Alberta, established in 1909, an organization that mixed a social brand of religion with politics. It was against this kind of cultural backdrop that some of the fundamentalists—united in their defense for a literal Bible, a premillennial eschatology, and personal conversion—became deeply concerned for the spiritual needs of the prairie people.

The Great Western Mission and Beulah Tabernacle
The Beulah Home and Mission in Edmonton, Alberta, began in 1910 under the leadership of Maude E. Chatham, a Mennonite Brethren deaconess. At the request of a group of people attending the Mission, the Alliance superintendent A. W. Roffe in Toronto, in August 1921, sent John H. Woodward to western Canada. He organized the Great Western Mission under The Christian and Missionary Alliance in

1922 during a visit by Superintendent Roffe. The first missionary convention pledge for missions totaled $2,800.

An old Anglican church building, seating only about a hundred, was purchased, and a Bible institute was begun in 1924 with 40 students. The students became pioneer missionary workers, conducting Sunday schools and church services in schoolhouses and halls.

E. J. Richards, then home secretary, presided over the Western Canadian District Workers Prayer Conference in 1925. The district was officially organized and John H. Woodward was elected superintendent. Students from the Canadian Bible Institute in Toronto were then challenged to spend their summers in the Great Western Mission. Encouraged by Mr. Roffe, evangelist Gordon Wishart arrived in the West to find that he and his coworker, Sid Pugh, would need some form of transportation to expedite their work. With $51.06 between them, they bought two saddle horses at Gwynne, Alberta, for $25.00 each, leaving them the balance of $1.06.

The young men contacted farmers and ranchers, presenting literature and a Christian witness. They conducted services in halls or schoolhouses whenever the opportunity came. Riding an average of thirty miles a day, they often slept in haylofts or schoolhouses. They were able to purchase bread and milk from farmers, fortunately balancing their diet by accepting invitations for meals along the way.

In 1927, Wishart, joined by a singing team, held meetings in the provinces of Alberta and Saskatchewan, moving a large tent from place to place by horse and wagon. In 1928, he formed a team with Welsh evangelist John Thomas and musician Elson Crosby, conducting evangelistic meetings in the larger cities of western Canada, including Regina. Superintendent Woodward desired to establish a branch in Regina and there Wishart contacted two families who had expressed interest in helping to establish an Alliance work.

Anxious to continue the evangelistic thrust, Woodward contacted Myrtle Bradley in Ohio to come to Regina. Wishart had seen a leaflet picturing Miss Bradley as "The Girl Evangelist from Ohio," and had a premonition that this was to be his wife.

The arrangement that brought Wishart and the girl evangelist together appeared to have been divinely ordained. After they were married they were instrumental in opening not only the branch in Regina but in Vancouver as well and in helping to open other cities in western Canada. When H. L. Turner opened an independent work in Saskatoon, the Wisharts went there to help, with the result that the first Alliance congregation was organized and is now known as Circle Drive Alliance Church in Saskatoon.

This is only one of many unusual stories that could be recounted to describe the vision and energies of those who labored in the West. But much of their success in pioneering came about through the impact of gospel radio broadcasts.

Impact of radio in the West

The long stretches of country between towns as well as the isolation of farmers and ranchers made evangelism difficult in the West. Ethnic communities were doubly hard to penetrate. The influence of the United Farmers of America, being both political and religious and with a strong social bent, blurred the secular-sacred distinction. Christian witnessing with only brief hit-and-miss contacts did not produce many converts, and it was even more difficult to disciple those who found the Lord.

Radio made its debut in western Canada in 1922 and became an effective instrument for breaking down the barriers of isolationism. One of the earliest radio preachers was William Aberhard who came to Calgary in 1910 as a lay preacher and high school principal. He began with a Bible class that ultimately became the Calgary Prophetic Bible Conference. The class attracted large crowds in the Grand Theatre.

In November 1925, Aberhard began preaching on radio CFCN which could be heard in Alberta, western Saskatchewan, eastern British Columbia, and in the northwestern area of the United States. Among visiting speakers was W. B. Riley, the fundamentalist leader and pastor of First Baptist Church in Minneapolis.

Aberhard's ministry was marked by plain gospel preaching, but his popularity gradually drew him into a mix of gospel and Social Credit politics. L. E. Maxwell, founder of Prairie Bible Institute in Three Hills, Alberta, had preached often for Aberhard but finally found himself opposing him for his dispensationalism and politics. Maxwell then began to broadcast his own program, so that ultimately his influence and that of the institute were felt throughout the West.

In Three Hills, Hector Kirk, whose daughters attended Nyack Missionary Training Institute, wrote to the Alliance requesting help in establishing a gospel work in the local school district. He was referred to W. C. Stevens, a former teacher at Nyack who had founded a Bible institute in Kansas City, Kansas, a school that existed only from 1918 to 1923. Stevens recommended the first and only graduate of the institute, L. E. Maxwell.

Maxwell recalls that Stevens said to him: "I wanted you here [to teach at the institute], but I think it would be better for you to be thrown on your own and learn firsthand the way of God for your life." Maxwell also said of the incident: "Unselfishly he surrendered me to the Kirks, and here I have been ever since." Dorothy Hill, former teacher at both Nyack and Kansas City, later joined Maxwell, continuing at Prairie until her retiral.

The keys to Bible interpretation for Maxwell were evangelization and missions. His close affinity with the Alliance view of sanctification increased general interest in the Society. Maxwell, however, would not identify with divine healing because he believed those who were not healed were often criticized for being weak in faith. His operation was geared strictly to interdenominational faith missions, and by 1975, that ministry had sent a total of 1,800 missionaries to the fields.

In 1927, Beulah Tabernacle was granted a license to broadcast religious services using the call letters CHMA. When the station was sold, broadcast time was purchased, and the Sunday morning radiocasts became a sort of "church home" for thousands of listeners. The radio ministry resulted in the development of Alliance work in Calgary, Red Deer, Lamont, Medicine Hat, Vermillion, Wimborne, Kindersley, Regina, Saskatoon, Winnipeg, Gwynne, Denzel, and Devon.

Evangelistic campaigns on the radio were a Canadian feature begun by Oscar Lowry, a former teacher in evangelism at Moody Bible Institute. He traveled from region to region, conducting six-week radio campaigns with unusual results. Invited by men from The Alliance Tabernacle in Regina and by Sinclair Whittaker of Briercrest Bible Institute, Lowry held a campaign from station CJRM, Regina, in 1938, with unusual results.

Lowry then went to CFCN in Calgary and had the cooperation of the choir from Prairie, including the time which Maxwell served on the same station. The closing meeting was conducted live from the Grand Theatre in Calgary, and 150 conversions were recorded. A follow-up meeting was attended by fifteen hundred persons at Three Hills, some driving as far as 400 miles. A similar campaign followed in Grande Prairie, Alberta.

A Canadian radio engineer once remarked that Lowry put daily radio broadcasting "on the map" in Alberta, and Maxwell confirmed that the campaign gave the institute the biggest boost it had ever received. While the war decreased the enrollment of students elsewhere, Prairie Bible Institute increased steadily.

Radio also played a significant part in the Beulah Church under the ministry of J. D. Carlson, a graduate of St. Paul Bible Institute. Carlson's personality and sincerity were suited particularly for radio and he is said to have had an audience of 500,000 for his program called "The Sunrise Gospel Hour." Some Alliance branches were organized as a result of his radio rallies.

In the late thirties Willis H. Brooks began his ministry in Regina, including the daily "Haven of Hope" broadcast. When Brooks invited George Blackett for a radio campaign, they agreed that a Bible institute was needed in Regina as a center for Alliance training in Canada. Blackett had been pastor of an Alliance branch in Owen Sound, Ontario, organized under Superintendent Oswald J. Smith. Then he served an independent church in Winnipeg and, as H. L. Turner had done before him, taught at the Winnipeg Bible Institute of which he was then dean.

The Canadian Bible Institute and the western expansion

In 1935, the Western Canadian District office was moved from Edmonton to Regina, with Gordon Skitch of Toronto as the superintendent. A new centralism was taking shape as the vision for Canada grew and flourished. The Canadian Bible Institute (now Canadian Bible College and Canadian Theological Seminary) was established as a training base in Regina in 1941. It began with about 50 students in the basement of the Alliance Tabernacle of which Brooks was pastor. Previously, many of the western Canadian young people who desired Alliance training had attended St. Paul Bible Institute in Minnesota or Simpson Bible Institute in Seattle, Washington. But now a sense of Canadian loyalty and conservation began to emerge.

One of the positive elements in this development was the training philosophy and vision for the church held by the Institute president, Mr. Blackett. He was not reluctant to identify The Christian and Missionary Alliance as a church and as a denomination. He also emphasized lay involvement in his pastoral methods classes. He encouraged young men to establish their call to the ministry and gave wise counsel wherever he saw need for it. Upon becoming district superintendent in 1954, he prepared handbooks for the training of church members and officers, as well as a catechism course which led to a junior church membership.

Sunday schools became an important factor in western Canada and their success was reflected in 1952 when Mavis Anderson of the Western Canadian District was chosen as the first Sunday school and Christian education secretary of The Christian and Missionary Alliance. The ambivalence of branch and church, hardly apparent in the West, disappeared entirely and a robust church has come into being, often referred to as a model for extension in The Christian and Missionary Alliance.

In 1949, the Beulah Alliance Church in Edmonton had 475 members and many adherents. Having outgrown its facility, the congregation decided to launch a daughter church. In the next two decades this Beulah family of daughter and granddaughter churches increased to seven with the mother church continuing its own growth as well. This pattern of church growth became a model to other older western city churches. In 1981, in the larger cities of western Canada, at least five churches could report nearly a thousand persons in single services, and about a dozen congregations reported attendance approaching five hundred. The largest church is Seven Oaks in Abbotsford, British Columbia, with a seating capacity for 2,300 persons and whose pledge to Alliance missions in 1981 was $174,000.

The large District of Western Canada was divided in 1964, and again in 1979. In 1980, the Western Canadian District, comprised of Alberta alone, had 66 churches; the Canadian Midwest District, comprised of Saskatchewan and Manitoba, had 61 churches; and the Canadian Pacific District in British Columbia had 42 churches—a total of 169 in the West. This reveals dynamic growth from the figure of 20 churches existing when the Western Canadian Bible Institute was established in 1941. All three districts were fortunate in having the creative leadership of Roy McIntyre as superintendent.

The Birth and Future of the Canadian Alliance

The coming to birth of a Canadian Alliance was a unique development. The strong combination of vision, responsibility, and accountability that prompted the mutual relationship of East and West for the whole of Canada would probably never have taken place without the basic anticipation of Canadian autonomy.

The beginning

The nature of the relationship between East and West became evident when Melvin Sylvester, a westerner who a short time before had become pastor of the Delta Alliance Church in Hamilton, Ontario, was elected superintendent of the Eastern and Central Canadian District; and when Melvin Shareski left a congregation of more than six hundred in Surrey, British Columbia, to become pastor of the First Alliance Church in Toronto, with only about sixty people in attendance. Relocated from the downtown area in 1977, it quickly grew from 60 to more than 400 in a few years.

Other good things were also taking place in the strategic city of Toronto. The Rexdale Alliance Church was becoming a growing, exciting fellowship of more than 600. Avenue Road Church, also hindered by downtown problems, relocated with 250 people in 1977 and grew quickly to more than 800. The East was on the move with nearly 70 churches in 1980 compared to 27 in 1950. All of Canada had only 99 churches in 1958: this number increased to 181 by 1973 and to 240 congregations in 1980.

God's providence was at work in many ways, and the tri-district conferences held in Regina in 1967 and in 1974 became the footings upon which the Canadian identity and autonomy could be formed.

The Chinese church

A continuing challenge to the Canadian Alliance, unique in many ways, is the Chinese church. As early as 1935, Ruby Johnston, with several friends, began to visit among the Chinese residents of Regina. A Chinese group first met in 1953, later calling Pastor Augustus Chao from Hong Kong. With assistance from Paul Bartel, former missionary to China and then dean at the college, the church was organized in 1961, with the distinction of being the first Chinese Alliance church in Canada.

Chinese immigration into Canada increased greatly in the 1950s. Then, between 1970 and 1979, a total of 138,260 Chinese students in higher education entered the country, and some of these became adherents in the Chinese Alliance churches.

Of 274 Canadian seminary graduates between 1972 and 1982, forty-four were Chinese. Forty-one have completed the undergraduate program since the first Chinese student was graduated from the Bible college in 1956—making a grand total of 85.

The mother Chinese church in Regina still has the most members—221, but several other churches promise to surpass that number. The church in Calgary, with its beautiful solar-heated edifice, is reporting an attendance of more than

450 with 70 percent of its nonmember adherents made up of Chinese students.

The Canadian Alliance now reports more than 20 Chinese churches in its fellowship. The first Chinese missionary convention of North America, patterned after the Urbana conference, was held in Regina in 1982 with nearly a thousand delegates challenged to reach "One Billion Souls."

Other ministries

Home missionary ministries in Canada also are expanding among Indians, Haitians, Eskimos, Vietnamese, and Japanese.

The most populated and needy area is French Quebec. For one hundred years the Roman Catholic church has controlled the religious life of its people there, but today those walls of solidarity seem to be crumbling. The Alliance began its outreach there in 1959, and in 1982 reported twelve French-speaking churches. The French language is used almost exclusively among the population of six million persons. If French leadership can be raised, the Alliance has an almost unparalleled opportunity for the future.

The Alliance constituency throughout all of Canada believes that all signs point to a promising future. The central education base is committed to training leaders for the church, both in the undergraduate student body of more than 400 students and in the seminary student body of 150. The headquarters has been established in Toronto in anticipation of rapid growth in the East, where the majority of the population is found.

12

The Alliance As a Missionary Church

While the average Christian church in today's society may not seem to have accepted missionary responsibility, within the heritage of The Christian and Missionary Alliance there is still the conviction that the highest and noblest calling God has given His church is missionary. Further, the lessons learned by experience indicate that there are no shortcut methods through which the church may quickly mature into a true missionary church.

Though struggles and changes have been many, the Alliance has kept to its original design of developing a missionary church—one where missionary interests and support are not divorced from the normal activity of the church.

Having served as pastor, missionary, vice-president of overseas missions, and president of The Christian and Missionary Alliance, Louis L. King made this observation in 1978:

When the Alliance was established, missionary endeavor from the United States was still young. Just 75 years had intervened between the commissioning of the first North American foreign missionary and the sending forth of the first missionaries by Dr. Simpson. The existing denominations, however, did not fundamentally structure missions into the church's life or into the whole structure of their theology. For them, missions remained a marginal concern at best and now in our day does not receive even the mild good will and commitment of a few years ago.

The Christian and Missionary Alliance, however, from its inception has been different. It has gone out into the world against the popular isolationist current and against the tides of denominational and cultural patterns.

Whatever else may identify the Alliance in its quest to represent Christ and His kingdom, this conviction that global mission is surely part of the church's normal life and Spirit-filled function is still the distinctive work of its calling.

The Universal Nature of Mission and Church

To insist that the universal nature of the church is missions is misleading. Rather, it is that a church of New Testament pattern will be able to reproduce itself anywhere in the world through its Christlike passion to save the lost and to bring new believers into Christian maturity.

There are those who do believe in overseas missions but show little concern for local evangelism. There are those, too, who claim that local evangelism is so imperative that they neglect the global mission of the church. Both are mistaken in a sense, for the two belong together, and it is this togetherness that places a heavy demand on the maturity of the church as a base for missionary operation.

The centrality of the church to a universal mission
Jesus said, "I will build my church." To fulfill His vision is the primary objective of mission. Christ is choosing Himself a bride and getting her ready for the final revelation.

It is common to hear the assertion that soul-saving is the "bottom line" in missions, but actually, soul-saving is not the final goal. Converts must be discipled and gathered into churches so that those baptized into the body of Christ come into a strong spiritual relationship both with Christ, the head of the church, and with every member of the body of Christ. Each missionary is not only a church planter but also a church builder. The church is not a mere fringe benefit but rather the goal of missions in history.

History teaches that not too many have clearly discerned the crucial necessity of church building in the missionary goal. The church has sent missionaries to evangelize, produce converts, and instruct them in the Word, but it has not always been faithful in follow-through—the founding and nourishing and maturing of churches.

Paul's concern as revealed in the book of Acts and in his letters to the churches was that the church and its members might grow up in togetherness in Christ Jesus. It was a pattern followed by the early church. Eusebius, writing early in the second century, describes the work of the twelve apostles:

> They performed the office of Evangelists to those who had not yet heard the faith, whilst, with a noble ambition to proclaim Christ, they also delivered to them the books of the Holy Gospels. After laying the foundation of the faith in foreign parts as the particular object of their mission, and after appointing others as shepherds of the flocks, and committing to these the care of those that had been recently introduced, they went again to other regions and nations, with the grace and cooperation of God (Eusebius, *Ecclesiastical History,* trans. Kirsopp Lake, book 3, vol. 1, Lake Classical Library; Cambridge, Mass.: Harvard University Press, 1975, p. 287).

When Dr. Simpson first launched the missionary society, the inroads of liberalism into the denominational churches inhibited the doctrine of the eternal damnation of all who had not heard of Christ. Social concerns and the promises of modern education and science were being substituted for the doctrine of lostness. Among the conservatives, the aim of missions was loosely defined, and the rapid conversion of the whole non-Christian world in the certain expectation of Christ's coming became the predominant theme.

During the first 40 years of Alliance missionary activity it was also common to operate orphanages, conduct industrial and boarding schools, establish farm colonies, build Bible schools, train evangelists and pastors, and build churches supported almost entirely from missionary funds. Generally, the missionaries were in control and neglected to employ a biblical strategy that would leave an indigenous church in order to allow missionaries to go "again to other regions and nations." Today, the planting and growth of the church as the body of Christ in the world remains the primary goal of missions, and social action is the result of the vision of the church and its saving effect upon society.

Feeding the hungry, caring for the sick and dying, and educating nations often are necessary to adequately establish a church, but as people learn to own the Lordship of Christ and live in the fellowship of the church as servants, social benefits become the fringe benefits of the gospel. Only as churches are established is the gospel effectively established and relayed to new regions and nations and the salvation which the church preaches involves not only the individual but society as well.

The calling of the church to a universal mission

God's people are called to a global mission. Generally, our foundation for missions biblically and practically has been far too narrow. God called Abraham and gave him a global promise:

"Leave your country, your people and your father's household and go to the land I will show you. I will make you into a great nation and I will bless you; I will make your name great, and you will be a blessing. I will bless those who bless you, and whoever curses you I will curse; and all peoples on earth will be blessed through you" (Gen. 12:1-3).

To Israel was given this word:

This is what God the Lord says—he who created the heavens and stretched them out, who spread out the earth and all that comes out of it, who gives breath to its people, and life to those who walk on it: "I, the Lord, have called you in righteousness; I will take hold of your hand. I will keep you and will make you a covenant for the people and a light for the Gentiles, to open eyes

*that are blind, to free captives from prison and to re-
lease from the dungeon those who sit in darkness"* (Isa.
42:5-7).

Just before His ascension Jesus said to the disciples:
*All authority in heaven and on earth has been given to
me. Therefore go and make disciples of all nations . . . .
And surely I will be with you always, to the very end of
the age"* (Matt. 28:18-20).

The view of the book of Romans is to look at Redemption
wholistically. God created a whole man and a whole world.
It was the whole man that sinned and a whole world fell under condemnation. So, too, it is the whole man and a whole
world that will come under the judgment of the final day. On
the other hand, it is the whole man redeemed that looks for
the resurrection and the whole world regenerated in which
Christ shall reign. *We know,* says Paul, *that the whole creation has been groaning as in the pains of childbirth right up
to the present time. Creation itself will be liberated from its
bondage to decay and brought into the glorious freedom of
the children of God* (Rom. 8:22, 21).

The book of Acts presents the growth and development of
a missionary church which began at Jerusalem and was
more perfectly fulfilled at Antioch. The design of the book is
to trace the transference of an old economy centered at Jerusalem with one that needed to identify with a global need as
seen from Rome, the seat of a universal empire.

The gospel is a global gospel. Missions gives a practical
dimension and reality to the gospel. The totality of a Christian's earthly existence involves the world; his faith environment includes both heaven and earth:

*And he is the head of the body, the church; he is the be-
ginning and the firstborn from among the dead, so that
in everything he might have the supremacy. For God
was pleased to have all his fullness dwell in him, and
through him to reconcile to himself all things, whether
things on earth or things in heaven, by making peace
through his blood, shed on the cross* (Col. 1:18-20).

The wholism of the gospel demands missions. The triumph of the gospel is a final kingdom on earth. Christ represented all men existing in Adam and He, the second and

last Adam, asks to be represented in every tribe, tongue, and nation.

It is a dynamic gospel that can save the stone-age tribesman as well as the learned university professor. It is a goal-oriented gospel: *this gospel of the kingdom will be preached in the whole world as a testimony to all nations, and then the end will come* (Matt. 24:14). Missions, therefore, is inherent to the gospel and to the nature of the church.

The operation of the church for a universal mission

Missions is a particular function of the church and needs to be distinguished from other essential but different functions. It has been noted that evangelism is a primary work in the church seeking reproduction and that its objectives are to reach the community as well as the ends of the earth.

In one sense, however, evangelism is that which is planned, promoted, and conserved in local churches through the witness of the members, while missions is that which sends out representatives from the local church to plant churches in other nations by pioneer evangelism. At the same time, whether it is the church at home or the church planted overseas, the believers must gather for worship, nurture, and fellowship of service and must be both evangelistic and missionary.

The Apostle Paul, as a missionary to the Corinthian church which he pioneered, indicated his plan clearly:

Our hope is that, as your faith continues to grow, our area of activity among you will greatly expand, so that we can preach the gospel in the regions beyond you. For we do not want to boast about work already done in another man's territory (2 Cor. 10:15-16).

Missionary expansion has a particular objective and a specific duty—to plant churches and to keep going after that which is lost.

The local church at home cannot be effective by being only missionary or evangelistic. It must be both of these, while worship, nurture, and service are kept in proper balance. The missionary, however, must look beyond the church that is planted and growing to the regions yet unreached.

The Apostle Paul reminded the Corinthians:

191

Apollos and I are working as a team, with the same aim, though each of us will be rewarded for his own hard work. We are only God's co-workers. You are God's garden, not ours; you are God's building, not ours (1 Cor. 3:8-9, TLB).

The church at Corinth belonged not to Paul and Apollos but to God as a garden that should reproduce, while Paul and Apollos should be free to turn new virgin soil for new gardens.

The strategy of missions is the multiplication of churches, and as churches are established the missionary must know how to let go and allow the church to accept its identity as an evangelistic and missionary church. This, however, is not accomplished quickly. The personnel of the mission overseas must work alongside that of the national church as coworkers without becoming lords over God's heritage.

The maturity that is best shown through a servant attitude by the sending church and the missionary overseas will largely determine what is being reproduced. If the Spirit-filled life is not being reproduced, the mission ceases to be dynamic, becoming institutionalized or fixated. The biblical warning, *without vision, the people perish,* is a sharp injunction when related to the church's worldwide mission.

To understand the biblical nature of a universal church mission is to recognize the need of spiritual maturity and stature for a base of operation. The Moravians had a motto, "The light that shines farthest shines brightest nearest home."

Actually, The Christian and Missionary Alliance has been a leader as a church devoted to world missions. Its history reveals a learning experience in becoming a missionary church instead of remaining a missionary society. It has been a pioneer in developing and refining the indigenous church concept and in the establishment of national churches. Its challenge of leadership has not been for pride or self-glory, but for a forward look to Christ's return when the harvest is completed.

To lengthen its cords the denomination must strengthen its stakes, even as Isaiah the prophet once advised:

Enlarge the place of your tent, stretch your tent cur-

tains wide, do not hold back; lengthen your cords, strengthen your stakes. For you will spread out to the right and to the left; your descendants will dispossess nations and settle in their desolate cities . . . the Holy One of Israel is your Redeemer; he is called the God of all the earth (Isa. 54:2-3, 5).

The Alliance Profile As a Missionary Church

A noted missionary statesman, Stephen Neil, made this observation of the 1980s:

On the whole the churches are very unmissionary, with small exceptions. This means the missionary is an isolated figure, unsupported by the weight of the church behind him (*Christianity Today*, Vol. 24, No. 13; July 18, 1980, p. 23).

God never intended that missions should be the task of an isolated missionary, but rather the task of every Christian within the church. The missionary is representative of the church's obedience, and only as the weight of the church is behind the missionary can its mission be fulfilled.

The home church as a missionary church

With the conviction that God's saving purpose is designed and addressed to the whole of creation as well as to the human individual, the typical member of an Alliance church does not think of his own salvation apart from God's whole family and God's whole world. He serves the body life of the church to find his highest calling with the gifts and the vocation wherein God has placed him. But whether or not God calls him to be a missionary or pastor, his vocation is surely a sacred calling because God wants His witnesses to demonstrate and testify of the grace of God in every walk of life, to be His church in visible representation in and before the community. Christ did not command all to be missionaries, but He did instruct not only the Twelve but also five hundred brethren at once in the principles of His commission.

The church as a discipleship enterprise for evangelism

and missions has a special function to bring balance and vision to the overall function of the gathered assembly. The pastor's concern for missions involves a recognition of the church's role and his preaching carries a missionary ingredient reflected in the gospel.

Ideally, every church has a permanent missions committee or chairman that stimulates missions education and plans all year for the annual missionary convention. As communication with missionaries is maintained and disseminated, prayer requests, information, and praise reports are shared with the church. The missionary policy of the church needs to be planned and workable under church board approval.

One special interest of the missions committee is the identification, recruitment, and shepherding of potential missionary candidates, giving them counsel regarding training and making available missionary books and biographies to read. With final church board approval, it sets goals for the amount of the next annual missionary pledge, appraises the possibilities of sending missionaries from the local church, and aims to interest various groups to take on approved specials on the mission fields. The goal is that every member of an Alliance church is involved in missions in some way so that the prayer and giving power of the church may be owned and blessed by the Lord of the harvest.

The essential watchword is *balance,* and a policy for missionary emphasis should fit the total priorities of the church's function. Commitment to missions may suffer from overemphasis as well as from underemphasis, and priority levels will change from church to church depending on background and context.

Essentially, the reason for missions involvement is the recognition of God's character and the fact that He has said that He cannot accept sinners unless they have been redeemed by the blood of Christ. God's love for the world is clearly related to His provision for this great salvation, and with unmistakable clarity His Great Commission involves every believer in missions. It is a plain and compelling doctrine that the sinner without Christ is finally and eternally separated from God.

Today, it is said that probably two and a half billion people on this earth still have no clear knowledge of the alternative the gospel represents. The time for harvest is now. There are about a thousand Alliance missionaries in countries overseas, but they represent only a token force in view of that which must be accomplished. We thank God for every evangelical missionary of whatever agency who is busy in seeking the lost, for the task is overwhelming. It is encouraging to know that the number of people being converted and discipled within a church in one year is a total that would have required many years of missionary effort previously. With an overseas church membership of about one and a quarter million, The Christian and Missionary Alliance in comity arrangement with other missionary agencies has been given responsibility for approximately 110 million souls—this indicating an almost stark reversal of the parable of the ninety-nine who were safe in the fold while only one was lost.

The national church as a missionary church

That God is building His church among many nations is cause for great rejoicing. The greatest potential of missionary endeavor is for every church, home or overseas, to be a New Testament missionary church even though its development probably will call for patient toil and sacrificial investment. An example of this is plainly seen in Viet Nam.

The missionary effort in Viet Nam began in 1911, with the first national conference held in 1924. By 1927, eight self-supporting churches organized into a national body. The early policy in Viet Nam was to establish churches with support of missionary funds but to withdraw 10 percent for each ten new believers in a given church—a policy later changed so as to make churches self-supporting from the start.

In 1930, this young church, in recognizing its own obligation to the ethnic minorities in the central Highlands, sent a national missionary to work alongside those missionaries from overseas who were pioneering among the tribal groups. As the tribal churches grew they, too, were represented in the national church committee. By 1941, 75 percent of the 121 congregations in Viet Nam were self-supporting.

Despite World War II and the war of independence from

the French (which continued from 1945 to 1954 when Viet Nam was divided at the seventeenth parallel), the church grew. National missionary work was enlarged among tribal groups and in 1961 a missionary couple was sent to Laos. By 1970, there were 368 local churches and 51,000 baptized members, 72 primary and secondary schools, a publishing house, a leprosarium, and 5 orphanages.

When the communists took over in 1975 and missionaries were expelled, there were 490 national churches. Under communist oppression since then, 100 church buildings are known to have been destroyed and 50 pastors have been sent to "reeducation" camps, while others have suffered in a variety of ways. No pastor has been able to move from the location he was in since the takeover in 1975. But in spite of the losses and restrictions, one church reported 1,000 converts in a year and a number of others are reported to be experiencing revival with increases greater than before 1975. The church lives on because the gates of hell will not prevail against it. A true missionary church is not a dying church even when missionaries are withdrawn.

Today, in at least ten countries, national churches raised up by the Alliance are sending approximately sixty missionaries to other countries even though there is still much to be accomplished in their own areas. In the Philippines, for example, The Christian and Missionary Alliance works in 26 languages and there are yet 74 other dialect or language groups that need to be reached. Yet the Philippine church has sent two couples to Indonesia. The Philippines, made up of more than 7,000 islands, has added four hundred new churches in five years, making a total close to 1,000. Similarly, Indonesia, made up of 13,000 islands with similar language problems, is a church that is baptizing nearly 10,000 believers a year. With a rapidly growing number of overseas Alliance churches, all of which are self-supporting and now numbering about 10,000, the potential for world evangelization is increasing.

From 1887 to 1960 the baptized membership reached 133,878; between 1960 and 1970, a total of 102,686 were added; and between 1971 and 1980 approximately another 150,000 were added.

Thus, the momentum for the harvest increases. The consistent missionary investment of The Christian and Missionary Alliance has produced much fruit, but the full results of harvest are only beginning. When Jesus said, *"All authority in heaven and on earth has been given to me. Therefore go and make disciples of all nations....And surely I will be with you always, to the very end of the age,"* the disciples at the time hardly realized what that could mean; but it represents the church's noblest and highest challenge.

The Christian and the Missionary in Alliance

The founder, A. B. Simpson, described the name Christian and Missionary Alliance to mean "we are an alliance of Christians for worldwide missionary work." In wry humor, A. W. Tozer described it as a name too long and awkward to handle without a pinch bar and that it required no prophetic gift to recognize that the present fellowship represented a magnificent triumph over bad nomenclature.

While the name was designed for a parachurch organization and the popular designation of "Alliance church" is somewhat inordinate, Christian and Missionary Alliance churches do represent Christians in an alliance for worldwide missions, though that is not the church's only function.

The needed balance and the denominational incentive

The design of the church is a reminder that neither evangelism nor missions was intended to be a solo performance. Both can be carried forward effectively only by team effort and must be the work of a fellowship where worship and nurture are adequately experienced and cultivated. Every member of the church and every organization and activity should have a part.

This is reassuring to the members who know that by themselves they could not possibly lead anyone to faith and spiritual maturity or fulfill the Great Commission. David L. Rambo, formerly vice-president/Division of Overseas Ministries, has commented:

197

As a former pastor, missionary and college president, I appreciate the unified ministries of Alliance missions. Where other missions and parachurch organizations offer attractive specialties, we also specialize; but we then concentrate and unify all specialties into one strong thrust to build the church of Jesus Christ. This is biblical and very effective.

The church is God's instrument to let the world know of the blessings God offers through His Son, Jesus Christ, and every member of the church is given both the obligation and opportunity to have a part. Neither missions nor evangelism represents an imposition because the very nature of being a Christian is to be a light to the world and to be like Jesus who gave His life for the world.

What Christians do in evangelism and missions depends much on the help they are given through their denominations. A local church by itself can be successful to a point, but what most churches do and how well they do it can be greatly increased through strong denominational leadership.

Because of every congregation's tendency to drift away from evangelism and missions, outside reminders are perpetually needed. Through leaders, publications, brochures, films, missionary tours to bring up-to-date reports from the fields, evangelistic conferences, and projects, vision and incentive are rekindled.

Paul the apostle used churches of other lands as examples that would set new standards for lagging work. He circulated letters of information among the churches. If he were alive in this generation, no doubt he would use the best means available to give vision and incentive to the churches.

The argument that outside help should be offered to autonomous local churches only when requested may be right in certain aspects of church work, but it cannot be right in terms of missions and evangelism. The churches that neglect such areas the most will be the least likely to ask for help. All churches need their motives prompted because nothing is fixed. Churches, and denominations as well, can learn from each other. Dr. Simpson's eloquent words bear repeating:

> We cannot afford to allow any sectarian spirit to cut

us off from the largest catholicity. We need our brethren of every Christian name, and it is still true, "Whether Paul, or Apollos, or Cephas ... all are yours." The whole Church of Christ needs our message and the inspiration of our spirit and work, and we need the fellowship and uplift of all saints. Let it therefore be our high ideal and aim and prayer that this blessed work may ever stand adjusted in all the will of God.

The larger and immediate perspective

As we understand the church and its role in the world from a biblical perspective, our hearts reach out in praise and trust in anticipation of a great harvest. Yet the need is so urgent that every Christian needs to take stock to reevaluate his priorities and relationships.

Approximately half of this world's population is still without the gospel, and most of the other half have never owned the true Lordship of Jesus Christ. According to an up-to-date mission handbook, the Protestant missionary force consists of 55,000 career and short-term workers of which 36,000 come from North America. Most of the other 19,000 come from the United Kingdom, Austria, Sweden, West Germany, Norway, South Africa, and Switzerland. It is estimated that the population of 4.3 billion in 1977 will be doubled by the year 2014.

Already starvation, increased earthquakes, wars and rumors of wars, and the threat of a world holocaust are upon us, and the biblical promise is: *And this gospel of the kingdom will be preached in the whole world as a testimony to all nations, and then the end will come* (Matt. 24:14).

The harvest is great not only in its opportunities but also in its difficulties. Cults, communism, secularism, extreme nationalism, and inflation are no small hindrances, but the greatest hindrance is the apathy of the church. Jesus said that all authority was His in heaven and on earth, and our availability to go, to pray, and to give in whatever capacity can remove any and all hindrances. When the church truly becomes God's instrument of working, ultimately nothing can stand before it because Jesus Christ is head of His church.

The history of the church in missions in the main is a history of great personalities and of missionary societies. Only in exceptional cases has it been the church in mission. The normalization of a more biblically designed program has been a relatively late awakening. The Reformation church was largely preoccupied with its own survival. German Pietism was the first to promote missions as "a church within a church."

The concept of a state church, however, dominated the European scene so that missions became bound politically. As the free church movement spread in England and America, most missions began as societies that functioned much like large corporations with support from individual Christians. This resulted in the misconception that missions was a mere adjunct to the church and the responsibility of individuals and groups rather than of churches. But the local church in relation to other churches in its fellowship together with the individual members of all the churches belong together organically in order to manifest full biblical truth.

The missionary is one sent under the authority, mediation, and delegation of the church. It is in the church and through the interdependence of churches that strength of proper mobilization and coordination is possible and that unity of purpose and action is provided for the missionary task. It is in this conviction that The Christian and Missionary Alliance cultivates its immediate and larger perspective.

Can and will The Christian and Missionary Alliance remain missionary?

Some contemporary missionary leaders remind us that, historically, the precedent of a denomination being truly missionary is yet to be established. The Moravians may have begun such a precedent in the early eighteenth century, if they can be called a denomination that kept its original calling, but The Christian and Missionary Alliance is setting precedent in evangelical missions. The annual missionary tour and convention-pledge system puts priority on missions. Expenses are prorated according to the amount pledged and monitored to give priority to direct overseas activity.

Historical studies reveal that the missions societies begun in the nineteenth century, and that were absorbed into denominations as mission boards, gradually lost the volunteer aspect of missions and began to operate on a percentage of the total budget. Missionary concern no longer received an adequate focus or emphasis.

The question arises: Since it has become a denomination, will The Christian and Missionary Alliance prove to be different? It does not have a separate mission board but professes to be totally missionary in its function. Continuing to teach and observe and carry out the biblical principle of missions is the basis of The Christian and Missionary Alliance's hope that it can indeed show forth that "difference."

13

The Alliance and the Relationship of the Local Church

Wherever church growth and development are being recorded, the "happening" is actually taking place in the local church, the fundamental unit in God's strategy for the evangelization of the world. In God's dealings with men there must always come the narrowing and deepening of His channel of operation in order that the blessing may be known worldwide. It is sad but true that when the local church falters, world evangelism falters; and when it strengthens its stakes and lengthens its cords, the circles of blessing enlarge and widen.

One of the most significant aspects of church doctrine is that God both blesses and judges the churches corporately. Paul wrote letters to churches as though he were addressing individuals. *I gave you milk, not solid food, for you were not yet ready for it. Indeed, you are still not ready. You are still worldly,* he wrote to the Corinthians. A few lines later he added, *For we are God's fellow workers; you are God's field, God's building* (1 Cor. 3:2-3, 9).

Again, he wrote to the Thessalonians: *You became imitators of us and of the Lord; in spite of severe suffering, you welcomed the message with the joy given by the Holy Spirit. And so you became a model to all the believers in Macedonia and Achaia* (1 Thess. 1:6-7).

The letters to the seven churches early in Revelation are

written as though they might be addressed to individuals, and the repeated phrase, *I know thy works,* and such exhortations as, *Remember the height from which you have fallen,* indicate the responsibility of individual churches and the importance of modeling or setting standards that effect strongly the universal church. And wherever the church assembles geographically, whether the one or the many, she exists as a whole, as "the church," because she is the church in that place.

Again, regardless of whether the apostles speak to individuals or to corporate churches, they are asked to recall their beginnings and their past experiences and thereby judge their present course. Paul exhorts Timothy:

Do not neglect your gift, which was given you through a prophetic message when the body of elders laid their hands on you.

Be diligent . . . Watch your life and doctrine closely. Persevere in them, . . . (1 Tim. 4:14-16).

John wrote to the church at Sardis:

Remember, therefore, what you have received and heard; obey it, and repent. But if you do not wake up, I will come like a thief, and you will not know at what time I will come to you (Rev. 3:3).

Churches, as well as individuals, must constantly be on guard against the danger of drifting. A world that does not accept the eternal Word of God will be shifting its priorities constantly, and again and again the church must take inventory of its values and course of development.

To understand my church with confidence of faith and intelligent concern is the best bulwark against historical drift. It is relatively easy to moralize that The Christian and Missionary Alliance is rapidly changing from an evangelistic, missionary, and deeper life movement into a stagnant or deteriorating institutionalism, without really understanding the significance of what has been received and obeyed and what it is that remains.

To accept negative moralizations without critical investigation and prayerful concern reveals an unawareness of what God in His providence has wrought in preparation for the final harvest. God has prepared His church for this day and believers are to own her with their highest and noblest commitment because God holds us responsible for this generation.

The Local Church in Perspective of the Whole World

The larger our perspective, the stronger and deeper will be our insights into the church's need. The Bible reminds us constantly of God's faithfulness in the whole of man's history. The prophets and apostles wrote and ministered as though they had a telescopic view, reminding their hearers that they belonged to the whole and that they were to see this world as God sees it.

Today, communications and travel seem to have made our world smaller, but its needs are still so great that we are frightened within our own relative security and comfort. What is the church's responsibility? Where does it begin and where does it end?

The dimension of the church's gospel

The premise on which the church is built is that the gospel is intended for all men. This is the starting point of the church's mission and there should be no hesitation or disagreement about that. The very nature of God and the nature of the gospel combine to involve the church in its mission to the whole world.

The church that identifies with a world vision can preach the gospel with great confidence. It is a gospel that can save to the uttermost whether it be the primitive tribesman or the sophisticated scientist in his modern laboratory. The risen Christ lives on to intercede for all.

The book of Acts reveals the New Testament emphasis upon the church's proclamation of the gospel and makes it plain also that the local assembly becomes the mediating and authoritative sending body of the missionary who is sent forth to represent the church in all the world. It is this stature and image the church, representing Jesus Christ, is to own. This is God's priority because Christ is head of the

204

church.

The church that identifies with a world vision can exercise a biblical faith for its vision of the gospel. To be adjusted and complete in all the will of God surely means the inclusion of both evangelism and missions. Whether we call the church a missionary church or an evangelistic church, we confess in essence that the gospel includes both, while in practice the distinctiveness of each must be given proper balance.

The danger of losing either evangelism or missions affects both the preaching of the gospel and the nature of the church. If everything is evangelism, soon nothing will be evangelism; if everything is missions, soon nothing will be missions. To strengthen the stakes and lengthen the cords simultaneously takes obedience and faith, but it is a design that God will bless and own for His glory.

The amazing success of the apostolic church was the result of a community of believers strongly knit together and lovingly committed to one another to penetrate the world for Christ. It was to the church that believers were added in Jerusalem even as witnesses from the congregation spread the Word to Samaria. It was the community dynamic of the church at Antioch that dispatched Paul and Barnabas as missionaries. Then, after their missionary journeys, they reported back the results to the same church. God does not simply select a Philip or a Stephen to evangelize or a Paul or a Barnabas as missionaries without a community of believers as their faith representatives to the world.

The church with a world vision has a perspective for its giving. The ultimate source of a church's giving power is not really measured by what the members can earn in secular employment, but rather by the nature of God's people whose vocations become sacred, owned and blessed by God.

The God who promised that through Abraham all the world would be blessed must channel His blessings in and through Abraham, even though he is occupied as a sheepherder. To bless the world, Abraham first must be a recipient. The church that is to bless the world by its obedience to the Great Commission will be the church that is first to be blessed. The *all power and authority* of Jesus Christ not only indicates spiritual power but refers to all the resources

God wants to generate in and through His people. This would include missionary personnel and money for missions. God will never be a debtor to His church because He gave His life for it and continues to do so.

The depth and the wideness of any church's strength will result from the vitality of that church's world vision. God will not be used for selfish reasons; but He rejoices in using His people to bless others.

The church with a world vision has a perspective for its hope. Jesus promised, *And this gospel of the kingdom will be preached in the whole world as a testimony to all nations, and then the end will come* (Matt. 24:14).

The aggressiveness of a church and the hope of a church are closely related. The imminence of the Lord's coming is more a matter of importance than of time. To be occupied with God's highest interests and noblest rewards adds such meaning to time that we look forward to Christ's appearing. Whether we are alive or whether we die before the Lord's coming are not the all-important issues; the issue is our faithful occupation in our own generation with the opportunities and privileges God has entrusted to us.

There is something ennobling, deeply enriching, and satisfying about a comprehensive gospel that is both preached and practiced. God desires the demonstration of such a gospel as background to its proclamation, and that demonstration and proclamation are to be centered in His church.

The dimension of the church's service

In the New Testament, the words used for service and for worship are almost synonymous. Our service demonstrates God's worthiness. The Bible speaks of the sacrifice of our lips and of a life of bodily service as expressions of worship. This takes on special significance when related to the dimension of building up the body for world service.

The Holy Spirit empowers the church for ministry both *in Jerusalem* and *to the ends of the earth* (Acts 1:8). In His omniscient sovereignty, He gives a variety of gifts to the church *to prepare God's people for works of service, so that the body of Christ may be built up,* marked by unity of faith and increasing maturity. Every member is said to be *joined and held together . . . as each part does its work* (Eph. 4: 12-16).

Only as the church realizes that all gifts and all members are indispensable to the life and service of the body, will the church serve most effectively at home or overseas.

Though separate missionary agencies seek to "serve" the church in many functions, they still operate independently as adjuncts to the church. On the field they cannot represent themselves as a mission of the church because they are autonomous, churchless missionary societies.

Because of an abnormal historical situation, The Christian and Missionary Alliance began as that kind of society, but with the development of a deeper and more adequate view of the church, the conviction has grown that the missionary nature of the church is essential to express adequately the New Testament pattern.

The missionary is to represent truly the home church's responsibility to the Great Commission. He is to represent the church's unity as being both organic and visible. He is to have the weight of the sending church behind him in prayer, in financial support, and in sending added workers as God's Spirit would appoint.

The missionary is sent overseas to plant churches—churches that bear the likeness, doctrines, and principles of practice that characterize the sending church. There is strength of worship and service in the proper mobilization and coordination of an interdependence that results in unity of purpose and action. In building up the local church as a pillar and foundation of truth through worship, nurture, evangelism, and missions the extended family of the Alliance is not striving for an impressive institution to magnify itself, but to magnify the Lord and to accomplish His work.

In its missionary operations, the Alliance has given liberty to each national church to direct its own affairs. In regard to church form, in things not commanded in the New Testament, the national church is encouraged to exercise freedom under the leadership of the Holy Spirit to suit the culture of the people. Each with its own distinctions, the sending church and the church planted overseas nevertheless work in harmony through mutual agreements. The missionary is a responsible representative of the supporting church at home and reports to the church, while the church overseas develops its own missionary ministry.

To keep this "world-service polity" in good order requires much wisdom and prayerful guidance from the Holy Spirit. Sometimes the argument is raised that it would be more economical to support national evangelists and pastors, rather than sending missionaries. Currently it costs about $10,000 a year to support one missionary, whereas a worker native to the culture would require no language study, no furlough, no large transportation costs, and lower living expenses. The argument also points to the rising nationalism that militates against the presence of foreigners, the isolation of living in a foreign culture, and the dangers that often attend missionary efforts. Why not change the strategy of missions and allow certain specialized missionaries to join the national churches while Western money might be used to help the churches abroad?

The answer is direct and simple: It is not New Testament strategy!

Missionary societies generally made their plans to go into a field with funds to erect mission compounds, convert some nationals, build a Bible school, and employ preachers and evangelists who would carry out the instructions of the missionaries. For them, this seemed to be the fastest and easiest way to accomplish the missionary task. Workers subject to a missionary employer would more likely do what the missionaries suggested. These societies presumed the work would grow as rapidly as converts were won, provided enough money was supplied from the church at home.

Such field arrangements brought many problems with only meager results, all of these conditioned by money. Advance on the field came to a standstill whenever political and economic conditions or circumstances prevented missionary presence. Instead of raising self-responsible leaders and self-supporting, self-propagating New Testament churches looking fully to the Lord as head of the church, missionary agencies cultivated hirelings and built deformed churches unable to reproduce.

The New Testament pattern insists that every receiving church is also a duly constituted church of Jesus Christ and that it is to mature through service so that the missionary may move on. The Holy Spirit can qualify and enable every constituted church to function adequately without continuous outside help. The first concern is not that the new churches are autonomous or indigenous, but that they represent Christ truly and have become dynamic in evangelism and missions.

Service as displayed in the New Testament is as much a divine means for Christian growth as it is a result of Christian maturity. Churches will grow and mature as they serve in love and dedication, and none should wait, expecting first to attain Christian perfection. This is true for Christians and churches at home as well as overseas. Gospel partnership in service for world evangelization is the strongest motivation and discipline for growth. This is worship with a practical as well as a spiritual dimension.

The commission to disciple the nations is an overwhelming assignment, and the ministry of the church is not finished until that assignment is completed through human instruments and mutual service. As the incarnation was necessary for world redemption, so personal identification in missionary service is necessary for the church. Partnership in the worldwide work of the gospel demonstrates that Christianity is stronger than national, political, social, cultural, or economic differences and that the gospel is mutually related both to Christ and to the whole world. Only the gospel of Jesus Christ is the absolute and final solution to man's universal need. Before the cross we are equals because its dynamic makes us one in Christ.

The Local Church in Perspective of the Community

The church's first and immediate responsibility is to the local community. The principle of *beginning at Jerusalem* (Luke 24:47) expresses the realistic nature of the church as being *the church of the living God, the pillar and foundation of the truth* (1 Tim. 3:15). Truth is to be expressed through real people, men and women who are bound together in their fellowship with Christ and with each other by common faith and purpose.

God has ordained that the Word is to be expressed in deed, the invisible is to be demonstrated in the visible, and the spiritually subjective is to be demonstrated by the materially objective. This is why the local church stands first and foremost in the work of the gospel.

The early church was influenced by a heresy called "Gnosticism," meaning "the knowing ones." This heresy has much that is common with modern existential philosophy. It taught that there was a great gulf fixed between the material from which all evil came and the spiritual from which all good came. Different forms of Gnosticism denied that Jesus Christ had come in the flesh; Christ only seemed to have a body or perhaps His physical body changed into a spiritual body at His baptism. This heresy was immediately countered in the book of Colossians and in the epistles of John. In his first epistle John wrote:

> *That which was from the beginning, which we have heard, which we have seen with our eyes, which we have looked at and our hands have touched—this we proclaim concerning the Word of life. The life appeared; we have seen it and testify to it, and we proclaim to you the eternal life, which was with the Father and has appeared to us. We proclaim to you what we have seen and heard, so that you also may have fellowship with us* (1 John 1:1-3).

To idealize a world vision of spiritual dimension without a realistic vision of practical dimension, or to spiritualize truth without experiencing it in real body life within the local church, is to fall into delusion and ineffectiveness so that others cannot find fellowship with us. Christianity is a religion of the Incarnation and the Resurrection supported by many infallible proofs of heavenly and spiritual realities. The temporarily invisible Christ now dwelling in the heavens is to be expressed in the body of Christ visibly.

The balanced life of the church's corporate faith

The world is to see demonstrated the truth of the gospel through the oneness of God's people. The Word preached and the Word demonstrated is a dynamic combination. Preaching is truth expressed through human personality, but not all members of the body can preach the truth effectively; however, all can demonstrate the truth in daily living. We live in a world that demands that the church earn the right to be heard, and when the church lives the truth opportunities to bear witness will multiply.

This is particularly true of believers corporately, because truth will be demonstrated from many perspectives when believers display their witness in unity. God wants the gospel to be represented in every legitimate vocation and the Bible exhorts a new convert to *retain the place in life that the Lord assigned to him and to which God has called him* (1 Cor. 7:17). God wants people of different capacities, backgrounds, sex, ages, and personalities to become a rich and persuasive demonstration of the gospel to an outside world.

Within the church the same differences, when anointed and gifted by the Spirit, will enrich and strengthen the church's body life and ministry. The corporate life within and without becomes a configuration that reaches the ends of the earth, magnifying a universal redemption by a sovereign Lord.

Paul wrote of the Thessalonian church:

You became a model to all the believers in Macedonia and Achaia. The Lord's message rang out from you not only in Macedonia and Achaia—your faith in God has become known everywhere (1 Thess. 1:7-8).

The effectiveness of the gospel preached is conditioned by the gospel demonstrated in a local church. The Bible claims the Word to be *living and active* (Heb. 4:12). The book of Acts demonstrates how the Word of God grew and multiplied through the church. Not everyone is gifted in seizing opportunities for communicating the gospel, but when priviledge and opportunity come, each believer is to witness to the gospel. Such witnessing is sustained and strengthened through the fellowship and encouragement of the church; this is part of the nature and design of the church.

The balanced life of the believer's personal faith

The corporate responsibility of the church does not diminish personal responsibility. Each believer is to be responsible to unite with a church or to be instrumental in developing a New Testament church when one is not present where he lives. The command "to disciple" means bringing the lost to Christ and gathering them into a corporate body through which worship, nurture, evangelism, and missions may be fostered.

The invisible nature of conversion is to be marked by visible baptism. The individual converted is to be the believer baptized and incorporated into the church in a mutual faith orientation. Here, again, the need of balance between the invisible and the visible and between the subjective and the objective is to be noted. The Great Commission includes baptism and applied learning:

> *Therefore go and make disciples of all nations, baptizing them in the name of the Father and of the Son and of the Holy Spirit, and teaching them to obey everything I have commanded you* (Matt. 28:19-20).

In the book of Acts a description of conversion is attended by baptism, with the assumption that believers had thereby been incorporated into the membership of the church, Christ's body (Acts 2:41).

> *The body is a unit, though it is made up of many parts; and though all its parts are many, they form one body. So it is with Christ. For we were all baptized by one Spirit into one body—whether Jews or Greeks, slave or free—and we were all given the one Spirit to drink* (1 Cor. 12:12-13).

The believer or church giving little importance to this visible provision not only hurts the convert, robbing him of the blessing of obedience, but also weakens the church. A convert will be only as strong as his identification with Christ and his commitment to Him, and his need is for a positive, visible identity with the body of Christ, revealing a newness of life in contrast to the world and his old life.

The invisible nature of fellowship is to be marked by visible communion. The character of the church is determined by its fellowship, first with Christ and then among believers. Fellowship in the gospel is primarily invisible, but at the Lord's table we express it visibly and its observance is to be preceded by self-examination (1 Cor. 11:28).

It is by the provision of the Atonement in Christ's body and blood, as symbolized by the elements of bread and the fruit of the vine, that reconciliation has been accomplished by the cross. This reconciliation to God is also to be represented by reconciliation among brethren because of the Savior's indwelling life that provides divine fellowship. The exhortation for self-examination at the Lord's table arose out of divisions and sects in the Corinthian church which had brought judgment upon the church (1 Cor. 11:18-19, 30). The example of the Corinthian assembly was in direct contrast to the church at Pentecost with its purposeful unity, a unity for which Jesus had prayed in His high-priestly prayer (John 17:20-23). Harmony and fellowship are made possible because of the Atonement.

The Lord's table symbolizes three specific things: (1) the finished work of the Atonement for which we are to be thankful, (2) the body of Christ and its communion for which we are to examine ourselves, and (3) the future deliverance to which we are to look forward.

In the synoptic Gospels the Lord's Supper is called the "passover." The Passover feast is a historic observance of the night Israel departed out of Egypt after the blood of the paschal lamb had been applied upon the doorposts to protect the household from the death angel, while inside the house a family and its guests partook of the roasted lamb. The Bible speaks of the Lord's table as symbolizing spiritual unity:

Is not the cup of thanksgiving for which we give thanks a participation in the blood of Christ? And is not the bread that we break a participation in the body of Christ? Because there is one loaf, we, who are many, are one body, for we all partake of the one loaf (1 Cor. 10:16-17).

The Second Coming of Christ is strongly set forth by the Lord's Supper. Jesus said to His disciples at the Lord's Supper, *I tell you, I will not drink of this fruit of the vine from now on until that day when I drink it anew with you in my Father's kingdom* (Matt. 26:29; see also Mark 14:25; Luke 22:18). In First Corinthians we are reminded that whenever we observe the Lord's table we *proclaim the Lord's death until he comes* (1 Cor. 11:26).

The harmony and fellowship of God's family in a local church is to be marked by the Lord's table. The invisible is to be expressed by the visible in order to make real the identity of personal responsibility.

The invisible nature of our consecration to Christ is to be marked by our visible service for Christ in and through the local church. This is clearly set forth in Romans 12, 1 Corinthians 12, and Ephesians 4. In Romans 12:1-2 the Apostle Paul exhorts:

Therefore, I urge you, brothers, in view of God's mercy, to offer your bodies as living sacrifices, holy and pleasing to God—which is your spiritual worship. Do not conform any longer to the pattern of this world, but be transformed by the renewing of your mind. Then you will be able to test and approve what God's will is—his good, pleasing and perfect will.

Christ expects to reveal His Lordship as head of the church through the personal consecration of believers. This fellowship is to serve bodily, even as Christ would serve on earth, and that more effectively because of the Holy Spirit's working in group dynamics. This is what Jesus meant when He predicted: *I tell you the truth, anyone who has faith in me will do what I have been doing. He will do even greater things than these, because I am going to the Father* (John 14:12).

Our motivational nature in consecration will be changed from a self-oriented life to a Christ-oriented personality; our adherence to social standards of right and wrong will be transformed by a renewed mind that is able to test and approve the will of God; and the Holy Spirit will have a profound impact on the personal life of the yielded believer, affording him love, joy, and peace.

The person who receives Christ into his life discovers an unknown potential for revolutionary change and effective service. The Holy Spirit begins immediately to shape and influence the believer's life, guiding him into a settled position of full consecration, by which he may avert a hopeless war between the self-life and the Christ-life. The fully consecrated believer will learn to yield to the Spirit, increasing the potential for effective service to others in the body of Christ.

Consecration without service is unthinkable, because the invisible will be marked by the visible. The context of Romans 12:1-2 reveals that Christians have gifts differing according to the proportion of faith (v. 6). As in our physical lives, when each member of our body responds to the head, so each believer is to respond to Christ, the head of the spiritual body. By the enabling and power of the Holy Spirit, the God-given gifts are to be exercised in worshipful service and proof of the good, acceptable, and perfect will of God. Christian service ought to demonstrate the Lord's wisdom and goodness as He enables that service to fit the believer's particular personality.

The church is God's idea. A. W. Tozer wrote:

One thing that instantly strikes the intelligent reader of the New Testament is the communal nature of the Christian faith. The social pronouns—we, they, us, them—are found everywhere. God's ideal is a fellowship of faith, a Christian community. He never intended that salvation should be received and enjoyed by the individual apart from the larger company of believers. The religious hermit is without scriptural authority or approval.

Many adherents to the church have neglected their membership responsibility simply because the church never took occasion to teach its own convictions. Often through its attitudes, the church appears to be saying, "Come if you will," or, "Stay away if you will." Understanding is the road to conviction and stability. As someone has aptly said, "Too often our candidates for church membership are welcomed upon a statement of their confusion rather than upon a statement of their conviction." Strong church members are those who understand with conviction their relationship to the church as ordained by God through the revelation of His Word.

The invisible balanced by the visible is the scriptural rule. Many passages of Scripture exhort the closest ties of unity among Christians and emphasize dependence upon one another, as well as necessary dependence on Christ. The Bible calls the church *God's household* (Eph. 2:19) and *the family of believers* (Gal. 6:10). It exhorts attendance and loyalty to the local church (Heb. 10:24-25), financial support of the local church (1 Tim. 5:17-18), cooperation with and esteem for the pastor (1 Thess. 5:13), and adherence to the discipline of the local church (1 Cor. 5:4-5).

To belong to this family does not mean approval of everything that is done there, but it does mean that because of the Christian's love and consideration of the needs and faults of God's people, *a multitude of sins* is covered (1 Pet. 4:8), that assurance of his transformation is established (1 John 3:14), and that his love for God is demonstrated (1 John 4:19-21).

The attitude of the Christian who insists on being footloose and fancy-free—attending church where and when he pleases, putting the Lord's money where his whims may decide, refusing the discipline of work and sacrifice for a cause that demands concentrated effort and patient endurance such as Christ revealed—certainly violates the clear teaching of God's Word. The Christian who sincerely seeks God's guidance will soon come to realize that Christ truly loved His church and gave His life for it and, therefore, those who would be Christlike should do the same.

Uniting in spirit, as well as in membership with the local church, is imperative to one's "unity" with Christ's body in doctrine, manner of living, behavior in the household of faith, and in all physical and spiritual responsibility.